The Drumbeat of Time

Also by Harold Klemp

Ask the Master, Book 1
Ask the Master, Book 2
Child in the Wilderness
The Living Word
Soul Travelers of the Far Country
The Spiritual Exercises of ECK
The Temple of ECK
The Wind of Change

The Mahanta Transcripts Series

Journey of Soul, Book 1
How to Find God, Book 2
The Secret Teachings, Book 3
The Golden Heart, Book 4
Cloak of Consciousness, Book 5
Unlocking the Puzzle Box, Book 6
The Eternal Dreamer, Book 7
The Dream Master, Book 8
We Come as Eagles, Book 9

Stories to Help You See
God in Your Life

The Book of ECK Parables, Volume 1
The Book of ECK Parables, Volume 2
The Book of ECK Parables, Volume 3
The Book of ECK Parables, Volume 4

MAHANTA

This book has been authored by and published under the supervision of the Mahanta, the Living ECK Master, Sri Harold Klemp. It is the Word of ECK.

The Drumbeat of Time

Harold Klemp

Mahanta Transcripts
Book 10

ECKANKAR
Minneapolis, MN

The Drumbeat of Time
Mahanta Transcripts, Book 10

Printed in U.S.A.

Compiled by Joan Klemp and Anne Pezdirc
Edited by Anthony Moore and Mary Carroll Moore

Cover design by Lois Stanfield
Cover painting by Georg Schedlbauer
Text illustrations by Fraser MacDonald
Text photo (page x) by Bree Renz
Back cover photo by John Jenkins

Second Printing—1995

Library of Congress Cataloging-in-Publication Data

Klemp, Harold.
    The drumbeat of time / Harold Klemp.
       p. cm. — (Mahanta transcripts ; bk. 10)
    Includes index.
    ISBN 1-57043-011-X : $14.00
    1. Eckankar (Organization)—Doctrines. 2. Spiritual life—
Eckankar (Organization) I. Title. II. Series: Klemp, Harold.
Mahanta transcripts ; bk. 10.
BP605.E3K5536 1995
299'.93—dc20   94-33534
                              CIP

Contents

Credit • Knowing What to Do • Purpose of Life • Becoming a Co-worker with God • What Is Spirituality? • Those Who Have Love • Opening the Heart • Recognizing Truth • Living a Life of Truth • Pushy • Ways to Give Love • A Spiritual Need to Fill

"Amazing Grace" as a Spiritual Exercise • Attitudes to
Avoid • Rewriting the Song • A Prayer to God

Foreword

The Way of the Eternal, *The Shariyat-Ki-Sugmad,*
Book One, states: "The knowledge that the true,
living Master gives is direct and immediate, coming from
actual Soul experiences apart from the physical senses
and human consciousness. His words are charged with the
ECK currents surging within him. They sink into the
inner self of the listener, leaving little doubt about the
existence of Soul experiences."

Sri Harold Klemp, the Mahanta, the Living ECK
Master travels in all parts of the world to give the sacred
teachings of ECK. Many of his public talks have been
released on video- and audiocassette, but others have
never before been available beyond the particular seminar at which he spoke.

As a special service to the students of ECK and truth
seekers everywhere, all of Sri Harold's public talks are
being transcribed and edited under his direction. Now
these transcripts can be study aids for your greater spiritual understanding.

The Drumbeat of Time, Mahanta Transcripts, Book 10,
contains his talks from 1990–91. May they serve to uplift
you to a greater vision of life.

Sri Harold Klemp, spiritual leader of ECKANKAR, speaks about awakening to ECK.

1

Dedication of the Temple of ECK

It's good to have a home. We've gathered here today for the dedication of the Temple of ECK and to transfer the Seat of Power to Chanhassen, Minnesota.

I wish everyone in ECK could have been here this morning physically. I know all of you who are here recognize this as a great privilege and an honor. But even as we sit here there are many who are invisible who have joined us. Other ECKists and the ECK Masters have come together for this singular moment in history. The dedication today, October 22, 1990, comes exactly twenty-five years after Paul Twitchell became the Mahanta, the Living ECK Master in 1965.

A New Direction

As the teachings of ECK began to reach out into the world, Paul recognized that the direction of ECK needed to move in a certain way. He recognized that there would need to be a place, a seat of power, to be the focus for ECKANKAR in its training of leaders—not just for his generation, but for generation after generation after generation. This was his vision. Twenty-five years later we are able to put another spiritual building block in place at this dedication of the Temple of ECK.

In 1971, Paul had a meeting in Las Vegas, Nevada, which was the Youth Training Council. Later, in August of the same year, a month before his translation, he met again with the youth in Long Beach, California. The reason he brought these people together was the need for leadership training.

I found it interesting how Paul opened the Las Vegas meeting in 1971. First, he read a list of the different religions or nations, their God or authority, and their seat of power. Talking about seats of power seemed an unusual way to open a weekend on leadership training. But Paul did it for one reason: because the Seat of Power is our link with humanity, and it must be a link that is directed by the ECK, by Divine Spirit. And the way to accomplish this is through the training of leaders who are versed in giving the teachings of ECK to the people.

Paul's Challenge

Paul ran into a situation back then. He simply didn't have enough ECK materials to give to the leaders in the early days of ECK. So a group in one part of the country would have a Satsang class, and since there weren't enough materials on ECKANKAR, they would begin to fall into spiritualism and other elements of the psychic path. Pretty soon that Satsang class was lost to ECKANKAR, because the people were no longer teaching the truth of the Sound and Light of God.

In the years since then, we have printed many books and discourses on the teachings of ECK. Since Paul's time, many of you have become Arahatas, or teachers, of the word of ECK, of the Sound and Light. Yet in the past twenty-five years, we have just *begun* to take the news of ECK into the world.

Past of Persecution

A Higher Initiate wondered why there seemed to be such a solitary nature among the ECK initiates today. She went in contemplation to the other planes, and an ECK Master was speaking. He said that in the past when the teachings of ECK were brought into the world, people who followed ECK were in a minority. Just to speak about the ECK teachings or the principles of Light and Sound opened them for persecution.

Many of you in the past had association with the teachings of Light and Sound at a time when you had to flee from the way people thought. The teachings of Light and Sound were different from the teachings taught in the orthodox churches, and those who followed ECK had to go underground to survive.

Community of Spirit

So the community of spirit that was originally in ECK broke into little pieces, as each person went here, there, and everywhere trying to survive. Instead of one cohesive ECK group, we became little pockets of individuals looking out for ourselves simply to survive. And this spirit has carried into the present time.

But now, with the dedication of the Temple of ECK, we again recognize that we are strong enough to bring the teachings of ECK to the public. And while we pursue this mission of bringing the teachings to the people, we have to learn this community of spirit all over again.

Unless we have this community of spirit, we are

3

always thinking about ourselves. When we're thinking about ourselves, we cannot give the love of God to others.

This is an important point in the spiritual history of earth, because the chelas of ECK are now together again.

Finding a Spiritual Home

At that 1971 meeting of the Youth Training Council where he listed a number of different nations and religions, Gods of power, and seats of power, Paul said, "Man has always placed the power or an altar of God someplace." This is one of those principles of truth which is all around us, but we often do not recognize the seat of power.

So Paul listed a number of them and then asked, "What do we do with the Seat of Power? Do we build a cathedral, a temple, an altar, or what?"

I thought it would be good today to listen to Paul as he spoke to the leadership, the ECK Youth Council, back in 1971:

ECK can never become substantially recognized as a group or as a power or anything until it has a place, a substantial place where the center of power is. I don't think this is a place to bring this up at the present time, but in the future we're going to come to that point in which we're going to say, ECK has a center of power in this particular place.

But where? And are we going to build a cathedral, are we going to build a temple, are we going to build an altar, are we going to do something else? We're going to have to think about this. I don't know when; we may have to think about it ten years from now, or we may have to think about it this year.

What I am striving for at the present time is as I was saying this afternoon—the purpose in bringing you in is to build a next generation of leadership. Then you're going to have to do something one day to build the next generation of leadership. This is going to have to go down and down and down and down until maybe a hundred years from now, when we are a substantial group of people.

What was Paul getting at during that leadership training?

His conclusion was that we can someday become a collective channel for ECK. Then the whole of this energy can flow through us, individually and collectively.

Missionary Era of ECKANKAR

Many of you have given your love and your gifts to bring about the Temple of ECK. With this Temple we can now begin the missionary era of ECKANKAR, to bring this new era of Light, love, and Sound to the people who are searching for truth.

We now have a home. We have a seat of power, a place where the collective energies of the chelas of ECK may come together and then go back out into life in a spiritually directed way.

As we work together, in love and harmony, we become an example for people. We are examples by our presence, by how we act and how we deal with others.

The list of people that I would like to thank for having made this Temple possible goes on and on. Thanks to the Board, to the Spiritual Council, to the Higher Initiates, to the RESAs, to the initiates of ECK. I would like to especially thank ECKANKAR's president, Peter Skelskey, and his wife, Sheri, for the time and the love they have given to make this Temple possible.

We have built a house. Now the great effort comes to make it a home.

Transfer of the Seat of Power

I would now like to go into the transfer of the Seat of Power from Sedona, Arizona, to the Temple of ECK here in Chanhassen, Minnesota.

Chanhassen is part of the greater metropolitan Minneapolis area. We'll be known as ECKANKAR, Minneapolis, Minnesota, because Minneapolis–Saint Paul is our home. The Temple is in one of the suburbs, Chanhassen, but we are in the greater metropolitan area of Minneapolis.

The date, October 22, 1990, is one of the most important dates in spiritual history. At this moment I would like to take the occasion to transfer the Seat of Power here to Chanhassen, Minnesota.

HU Is for Everyone

For the future, we have a videocassette, *The Temple of ECK: A New Golden Age.* Because history is happening and we are in the middle of it, it's easy to overlook the significance of today. But I'm happy you could come to this special ceremony as we now begin, in earnest, our mission of carrying the Light and Sound of ECK to the world.

As we go into the world to carry the Light and Sound of ECK, remember to take the sound of HU to the people. It helps them so much.

HU is for everyone, whether or not they belong to ECKANKAR, whether or not they know it is connected with ECKANKAR. Whenever you have the opportunity to give it to people in need, please do so. They may not understand spiritually during the moment you are doing this, but they will later.

So, welcome to the new home of ECKANKAR. Thank

6

you very much for coming, and sharing, and being here on one of the most important and joyful days I've ever had in ECKANKAR. May the blessings be.

Dedication of the Temple of ECK,
Chanhassen, Minnesota, Monday, October 22, 1990

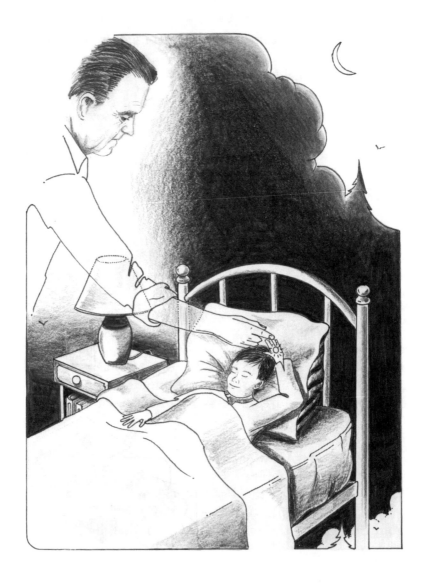

In the dream, the traveler came to him and held up the silver dollar. Then the boy woke up, and the silver dollar was in his hand.

2

The Silver Dollar

The dedication of the Temple of ECK in Chanhassen, Minnesota, on October 22, 1990, was a special event in the history of ECKANKAR. I wish all of you could have been there physically.

In ECKANKAR we often make the distinction between being somewhere physically or nonphysically. Other people might wonder what we are talking about, but this is a reality for our path. We know that we can have an experience in the dream state in a place far from home. Others who have a similar experience might say it was just a dream.

In ECKANKAR we are dealing with a different reality. We find that there is a connection between our everyday life and what others would call dreams. Life is a continuum that goes on without interruption, not only from the past to the present, but from one plane to another.

Nimble State of Consciousness

To be able to accept the changes as you move from the present to the future, or from one plane to another in the present, requires a very nimble state of consciousness. Many people are not aware, except in the barest fashion, that they even have a state of consciousness. If you were to point out to them that they had one, they would simply say, "Well, yes, of course."

No one wants to hear that their state of consciousness is not very nimble. People get defensive at the mere suggestion. Even while denying such concepts as the reality of the dream worlds or reincarnation, they actually feel that they are open to the pulse of life.

But, then, we all have our illusions. While we might see ourself as bright and aware, the friends who know us well would probably say, "We don't want to speak badly about him, but . . ."

What Are Obstacles?

As the Temple of ECK came closer to completion, we ran into problems at every turn. The building inspectors found one requirement after another that had to be satisfied before they would issue an occupancy permit. The delays seemed endless. We were making adjustments right up to the week before the dedication.

At first we thought the dedication would take place as early as July. We moved it to August, then September. Finally it became apparent that the dedication of the Temple of ECK should take place on October 22, which marks the new year in ECKANKAR.

This was the natural process. The obstacles were actually things that the ECK, or Holy Spirit, put in the way to make everything come out correctly in the end, including the date of the dedication.

Everything works out for the best when the ECK is in charge.

Seats of Power

At the dedication we played an excerpt from a recorded talk that Paul Twitchell gave at a meeting of the Youth Training Council in March 1971, about half a year before he translated. His words were most appropriate for this very special event in ECK history.

Paul began the leadership training session in a very unusual way: He cited a number of different Gods of power and seats of power established by nations and religions throughout history. The United States, for instance, recognizes a God of power or an authority figure. The U.S. authority is vested in the president, whose seat of power is Washington, D.C. In England, the authority is vested in the head of the royal family, the king or queen, and the seat of power is in London. Seats of power change as history changes.

Paul then went into the different religions, such as Buddhism and Christianity, which also have their God of power and their seat of power. With the rapid growth in membership, he recognized that ECKANKAR, too, would someday need a Seat of Power. Because unless an organization had a center of power, it would not be recognized as a force in the world.

We now have a Seat of Power. The religion is ECKANKAR, the God of power is SUGMAD, and the Seat of Power is located in Chanhassen, Minnesota, in the Minneapolis area.

A New Feeling

As time goes on, there will be a totally new feeling to ECKANKAR. With the Temple of ECK, we now have a home.

I can't explain how important this is. To put it as simply as I can, the Seat of Power is our connection with the world. It is the center from which the message of the Light and Sound of God will go out to the world. It is also a place where the initiates can come to learn how to be leaders in ECK.

Building Leaders

Paul went on to tell the ECK Youth Council about the need for leadership training. He said the present generation of ECKists would have to train the next generation of leadership. They would then train the next group, and so on. This could go on for a hundred years, he said, or until we become established in this world.

He recognized that it wasn't going to happen in five, ten, or even twenty-five years. It takes a long time to establish something like ECKANKAR. It also takes doing the right things, such as establishing a Seat of Power.

So many new things are happening in ECKANKAR now. Besides the dedication of the Temple of ECK, this seminar also marks the beginning of the Year of the Vahana, the ECK missionary, as well as the twenty-fifth anniversary of ECKANKAR. Since silver is the symbol for a twenty-fifth anniversary, I thought the next story was very appropriate.

The Silver Dollar

An ECKist told me about a silver dollar, given to him when he was eight years old. He lived on the East Coast, where his parents had a rooming house. One day a traveler passed through. He was an interesting person, but he seemed to be down on his luck.

The boy had just received a silver dollar for his birthday. His uncle had given it to him, telling him to keep it because it would be valuable someday. But the boy decided to give it to the traveler, even though the man had never asked for money. "You need it more than I do," he told the man.

Sometime later, when the boy had grown up and found ECKANKAR, he recognized this man as Paul Twitchell.

Yet as a boy he got into trouble for giving away his birthday present. When he told his mother he had given it to the traveler, she scolded him for being so foolish. He felt very bad.

A few weeks later the boy had a dream. In the dream, the traveler came to him and held up the silver dollar. "It's very precious, isn't it?" the man asked. The boy nodded. The man put the silver dollar into the boy's hands in the dream. "Now hold tight," said the man before he disappeared.

Then the boy woke up, and the silver dollar was in his hand.

Game of Life

The boy remembered how the man had often played checkers with him.

The first time they played, the game was over before the boy knew it. The traveler was a very adept player and won easily. "Checkers is like the game of life," he said. "I'm going to show you how to play it better." They set up the board again and began a new game.

The boy moved one of the checkers. "Now look where you put that piece," the man said. "You moved it here because you knew what you wanted to do. But you also have to anticipate what I'm going to do. And now that you've taken your finger off the checker, you can't do anything else until I make my move."

This is how the game of life is played. We are responsible for whatever we do. According to the Law of Karma, any act we perform sets something in motion. If you move a piece on the game board of life, then you have to wait until somebody else takes their turn. We're all playing the same game, and it helps if you know what moves the other person might make.

Then, once they make their move, it's your turn again, and you have to know what you're going to do next. You have to look at all the possibilities. If you move your piece to a certain point on the board, how will the other person respond? How will their response affect you?

"I want to show you something else," the man said. "When you moved your checker, notice how you boxed yourself into a corner." The boy studied the board, and sure enough, he was boxed in a corner. "Now you're going to have to pay the price to get out of there."

When the boy made his next move, he lost a couple of his checkers. That was the price he had to pay for not leaving himself a way out.

Paul, who was just passing through the area at the time, was already preparing for the Mastership he was to take in a few years. Even then he was teaching.

Recognizing the Master

As the years passed and the boy grew up, he often thought about the silver dollar. He tried to think of ways he might have gotten it back; he realized the easiest thing would be to accept that the man in his dream had given it to him.

The young man came into ECKANKAR in 1971, just after Paul Twitchell translated. When he saw pictures of

14

the founder of ECKANKAR, he recognized him immediately. "That's the very same man who stayed in my parents' rooming house when I was a child," he said. "He's the man who gave me back my silver dollar in the dream!"

Giving Back

In spring 1990, during the construction of the Temple of ECK, the man visited the Temple. Looking at the foundation of the Temple before the concrete was poured, he very carefully pressed his silver dollar into the earth of one of the unfinished rooms.

Years from now, workmen doing repairs on the basement floor of the Temple will come across this silver dollar. "Someone must have dropped it when they built this place," they'll say. But it was not dropped accidentally—it was placed there with love by someone who had learned many lessons from a silver dollar—lessons that went all the way back to the early days of Paul Twitchell, the founder of ECKANKAR.

Gateway to Heaven

On Monday, October 22, the day of the Temple dedication, this man was contemplating in the same room. Suddenly he looked at the wall and saw shimmering light like the transporter beams from the TV series *Star Trek*.

Through this gateway into the heavenly worlds, he saw a group of ECK Masters coming to the Temple for the dedication. He could hardly believe his eyes. After most of the people had come through, Wah Z, the Inner Master, came in.

Then the last person came through the gateway. It was Paul Twitchell.

15

Paul walked up to one of the walls in the room and scratched the paint a little with his fingernail. The man heard him say, "Hmmm, better than I imagined." Then Paul walked upstairs.

A few minutes later, I came into the room physically. The man told me later that I walked over to the same spot that Paul had scratched, stared at it for a while, put a hand to the wall for a moment, then walked out. The man was amazed. Later he asked his wife, "How did he know?"

We don't tell everything.

One Small Thing for Love

I got a letter from a woman who was pretty fed up with the way things were going. Life had caught up with her, sat on her, then stomped her down. She just didn't know what to do. "Harold, tell it to me straight," she wrote. "What do I need to know?"

If someone finds it difficult to work out their problems and let's say you know it's because they are out of balance, the worst thing you can do is to tell them so directly. To say, "You are out of balance," does them no good whatsoever.

In my early days in this position, I sometimes tried to help people by telling them very directly what their problem was. The people might have thought they wanted to hear this, but actually they did not. They weren't able to handle it. Things got worse instead of better.

I have since found that it is best spiritually if I give people ways to make things better from the ground up. There might be a hundred different problems in the person's life. Instead of wondering which one to tackle first, I ignore the problems. I try to show them the way of divine love.

Love cuts through all this stuff. I mean this sincerely. Love is the shortcut to heaven.

People in other religions have many different practices—prayer, saying the rosaries, and so on. In ECK we do a contemplation or spiritual exercise. These are all good practices. But in some of the religions, people have forgotten why they are doing these practices.

The only reason to do any of these religious practices is to find divine love. Then one can become a being of light and love in the world. That is the only purpose. If people practice anything that is not intended to make them vehicles of light and love, then it is a worthless practice.

Responding to the woman's letter, I simply wrote, "Do one small thing for someone else each day. Do it for love and love alone, and expect nothing at all in return."

She later wrote to tell me how excited she was when she opened her mail. Wanting to tell someone about it, she called a friend and said, "Hey, Harold actually reads these letters. He wrote back to me!" Then she asked her friend, "Can you meet me at the mall for a snack?"

"I'd really like to," the friend said, "but I can't. I have to go to a meeting."

The ECKist was disappointed. The letter had opened the love inside her, and she wanted to share it with her friend. But the ECK, the Holy Spirit, doesn't always arrange things exactly the way you want.

Giving in a Humble Way

The letter had said she was to do one small thing for someone else each day, and expect nothing at all in return. Filled with the love of God, it would have been too easy to babble her love away over a snack. Without realizing it, this is what she'd wanted to do—spill it across the

17

table to a friend. There would have been nothing wrong with that, but the ECK wanted to teach her how to give love in a more humble way.

The ECKist went to the mall alone and treated herself to a milkshake. Too excited to go back home, she went outside and sat by the fountain in the courtyard. There were birds everywhere. How nice it would be if I had some bread to feed them, she thought.

Just like that, from out of the sky came this chunk of bread. It hit her on the shoulder and fell to the ground in front of her. "Heaven does provide," she laughed. She didn't know where it had come from, but she accepted it. Picking it up from the ground, she broke the bread into little pieces and fed it to the birds.

The ECK was showing her a way to do one small thing each day for love and love alone, with no expectation of reward. The birds couldn't give her anything back, whereas her friend might have been able to. It was as if the ECK had said, "Here are the birds, and here's the bread. Now take what you have, and figure out what to do."

Life's Gifts

This was her spiritual exercise, and it's the spiritual exercise I'm leaving with you. It can be used by a Christian, a Buddhist, a Moslem, an ECKist, or anyone else. No matter what religion or faith you observe, you are doing something for one of God's creatures. And you are doing it with love, with no expectation of reward.

After she fed all the bread to the birds and went home, her friend called and said, "The meeting was canceled. We can have lunch after all." So everything turned out as she had planned originally, but more so.

As you do one little thing each day for love and love

18

alone, without any expectation of reward, you are going to find that life gives you more and more.

ECK Worldwide Seminar, Orlando, Florida,
Friday, October 26, 1990

"Take this money to your mother," he said. "Tell her it's to buy you that toy and the rest is for her."

3

One Hundred Dollars

The Temple of ECK is a gift to the world. Even people who come there who are not in ECKANKAR say there is such a feeling of peace. The entire area has a presence; and as time goes on, people will put better words to it. It's the Holy Spirit, the ECK, manifesting Itself.

The Temple is a connection between ECKANKAR and the world. It's a special building, for a special purpose, in a special time.

Was That Experience Real?

This weekend I talked with several people who have had experiences in the inner worlds, through dreams or in a more direct way, such as Soul Travel. One individual said he still wondered, Was that experience real?

At first he knew it was real, but then he shared it with other people who, with no knowledge of the inner worlds, raised doubt. "Are you sure it was real?" they asked. All of a sudden the person wasn't so sure anymore.

Those who love life, who are the true members of any religion, know the reality of this life, the next life, and the lives that follow. This is what we are trying to show in ECKANKAR.

Direct Path

Someone asked me today, "Is ECKANKAR the only path?"

"No," I said, "but it is the path that helps an individual most directly become conscious of life and the different levels of existence."

This was important to her. In the years she had been in ECKANKAR, she often had felt that some people were not in touch with reality.

In any religious or philosophical group, you find a range of people—from the very practical to the completely whimsical, and a small number who have no connection at all with reality. One hopes, of course, that most of the people are compatible with the basic nature of the group.

ECKists today are more practical and down-to-earth than they were in the past. This is necessary. It is our spiritual philosophy that heaven is here and now, in this moment. Therefore, the spiritual lessons that we have to learn are right here, in our present life.

One Hundred Dollars

A Higher Initiate told me that many years ago, as a seventeen-year-old high school student, he went around asking his friends, "What would you do if I gave you a hundred dollars?"

I thought it was a peculiar question. When you're dealing with a theoretical situation, people usually tell only their noblest thoughts. Their generosity to charity would make a saint cry. After all, they're not risking anything. It's imaginary money, and their use of it is hypothetical.

If he actually gave someone the hundred dollars, he probably wouldn't see them again until it was all gone. Then they'd come back and say, "Hey, thanks a lot. That was really great of you. When can I have another hundred?"

He interrupted my reverie to tell me some of the responses his friends had given. One said, "If you gave me a hundred dollars, I'd use it to throw a party. I'd invite a lot of friends over, and we'd all get drunk and have a good time." I guess you could call that a form of sharing.

Others were completely selfish; they'd use the money for a dress, a suit, electronic equipment, a down payment on a car.

He presented this question to a lot of his friends over a long period of time, and their answers were mostly self-serving. Most talked about what the money would do for them; some even said they'd use it in ways that were actually destructive or dimmed the consciousness.

A Special Friend

Even back then, this individual had begun to have inner experiences. One day he shared them with another friend, a very special person who had spent some time in the state asylum. "Hey, don't talk about things like that," his friend said. "If you keep it up, they'll put *you* away."

There has been a rise in spiritual consciousness in the world since then, of course. But twenty or thirty years ago, it was not common for people to talk about such things as near-death experiences. These days, you hear about them everywhere. Movies and TV shows employ special effects to create the illusion of beautiful tunnels of light. The scenes are so vivid that you sometimes wonder if heaven could be better than these staged productions.

The individual then decided to ask his friend the question: "What would you do if I gave you a hundred dollars?"

23

"I would give it away," the friend said. "I would look and look until I found just the right person—someone who would give it to somebody else who needed it more."

Repaying a Loan

"Whatever made you ask such a question?" I said. "It's unusual enough that you even came up with it at such a young age. But the fact that you spent so much time on it and persisted for so long is quite extraordinary. Why did you do that?"

He then told me the story behind the story. Several months before he began to query people about how they'd spend the one hundred dollars, his mother had asked him to lend her some money. A hardworking young man, he was very careful with his money, faithfully putting most of it in the bank. But his mother promised to pay him back by a certain date, so he willingly loaned it to her.

A few weeks later he said, "Mother, remember the money you borrowed from me? You said you would repay it. Are you going to do it soon?"

"Oh, I thought you were giving me a little extra in addition to the rent money," she said.

He didn't know what to make of this. He loved his mother and had trusted her.

Later he asked her about it again. "When you borrowed this money, you told me you would pay it back." This time she gave him another excuse, entirely different from the first one.

The reasons his mother gave for keeping the money were not the truth. When he realized that she was never going to repay him, his faith in her was destroyed on the spot. He had loaned the money freely. Having a promise broken by someone he loved so much, his own mother,

24

made him lose something special in his heart.

A Dream Realized

After he finished this part of the story, we were quiet. Then, being a very pragmatic person, I said, "So far we're talking about what people would do if they were given the money. We haven't seen proof of anyone with a real hundred dollars in his hand. I wonder what would happen then."

So the ECKist went on to finish the story.

Later that year around Christmastime he was in a department store, just watching the people. All around him the shoppers scurried about, stopping here and there to buy presents or just to look. Some had enough money, others didn't.

He noticed a woman with her little boy. He looked to be about five or six years old. The mother was dressed in very poor clothing, and he imagined she was probably a single parent. Things were harder in those days for a woman who had a child and then had to try to make a living.

The boy stood in front of a toy display counter and looked longingly at something behind the glass. "Mom, could I have that toy?" he asked.

"We don't have enough money," she answered. Her tone was bitter. She wanted to get the toy for him, but she just couldn't afford it.

"Maybe Santa Claus will bring it," he said hopefully.

"There is no Santa Claus," his mother said. There was a hard edge to her words, the kind that comes from having a child who depends on you, but not being able to care for him as you would like.

The young man who later became an ECKist watched the mother wander a little farther into the store. The child turned back to the showcase and pressed his face against

25

the glass. He stared at the toy with a look that seemed to say, "That's a dream I'll never see."

This is where the story finally went beyond the hypothetical. The young man went up to the little boy and put a $100 bill in his hand. "Take this money to your mother," he said. "Tell her it's to buy you that toy and the rest is for her." With that, he moved away from the boy and blended in with the crowd, watching to see what would happen.

The boy ran through the store to find his mother. Waving the money in front of her, he said, "Mommy, now you can buy me my toy!"

His mother looked shocked. "Where did you get that?" she demanded to know.

"A man gave it to me," the boy answered. "He said it's to buy my toy and the rest is for you."

The mother's eyes scanned the crowd. She didn't spot the young man who was watching her, but she quickly made up her mind to accept this new turn of events. Grabbing the boy's hand, she marched back to the toy counter, plunked down the money, and bought him the coveted toy.

Restored Faith

"What would you have done if the mother hadn't bought the toy for the child?" I asked.

"I would have gone up to her and said, 'Excuse me, that money's mine,'" the ECKist told me.

Many years ago this man's own mother, without realizing it, almost broke his dreams and his faith in people. Luckily she didn't quite succeed. That Christmas, he saw that the only thing that kept the boy from his dream was a certain amount of money. He knew he could do something about it.

But he also made it into a test of sorts. Was the boy's

26

mother an honorable person? Yes, she was. Her actions restored the young man's faith, and I suspect it turned out to be a very happy Christmas for both mother and child.

This was a good example of a person who puts his money where his mouth is. It is also the story of someone who had truly given. But more than just giving a hundred dollars, this young man was building a dream.

Whenever you give a gift to someone, it has to be given with no strings attached. You must give it without ever expecting a return. But it must be a gift that builds dreams and lets people grow.

Giving Divine Love

Last night I said to do one small deed of love without expecting anything in return. The spiritual exercise for tonight is: do it twice. Two times each day, do one small thing for someone else, without expecting anything in return.

As you do this, you are giving divine love. You are being a channel for God. You are being a missionary for ECK, for the Holy Spirit.

To be a true missionary for ECK means to give divine love to other people. It is a poor missionary who goes out among the people of the world to build his own dreams. A true missionary brings people a gift that builds their dreams.

Help Build People's Dreams

In this Year of the Vahana, many of you are going to be on missionary teams. As you carry the Light and Sound of God to others through the teachings of ECK, remember to build their dreams, not yours.

How do you do this? I think you'll know. When you are in a situation where it comes up, all of a sudden you'll realize that you are being a channel for God.

This will often happen when you least expect it. You may be at work, relaxing with your friends, or at home with your family. Some little thing will come up. This is the time to do one small act of love for someone else and expect nothing in return for it. This is being a true missionary for the Holy Spirit.

Goodness

Several people have mentioned a contrast between a past seminar here in Orlando and this one. Some have observed a difference in the audience this time. The way one person expressed it, "There is a feeling of goodness that wasn't here in the past." It is because of the Temple of ECK. With this connection between ECKANKAR and the world, something's happening.

ECKists are finding out that it's OK to be charitable, to love people, and to do something for others. But you don't need praise and recognition from others for the things you do for ECK. Spiritually, your reward will come to you many times over.

People who give to others find that they have better health and enjoy a happier life than those who have yet to learn the blessings of giving of themselves. And the giving is usually better when no one knows you've done it. You have the quiet satisfaction of knowing that you have acted as a channel for God. No one knows except God—and God knows.

ECK Worldwide Seminar, Orlando, Florida,
Saturday, October 27, 1990

28

On top of a nice discount on the hanging plant, she threw in the marigolds for free. The clerk probably didn't realize that she was involved in spiritual giving.

4

Food, Co-worker, and Other Things

I would like to touch on a few topics that will help you live a better, more meaningful life in ECK. Some of you will detect a very direct connection to what is happening in your own life; others might have to think about it for a while.

One thing you can do is watch the foods you eat as an aid to a better spiritual life. Many of you commented on a talk I gave about my own reactions to certain foods.

Monday Sickness

One woman found it of particular interest because of the effects of food on members of her own family. When her oldest son was in the sixth grade, he always got sick on Monday mornings. "He has school phobia," his teacher said. "Just give him a tranquilizer and send him anyway."

People who deal with unruly children often consider this a solution. Instead of trying to identify the problem, they find it easier to just ask the doctor for medication to tranquilize the child. Even an educated person like this boy's teacher, who should have known better, babbled on about school phobia and drugs.

But the mother knew this was not the answer. The still small voice of the Mahanta had spoken to her. "Look a little bit further," it said.

Suspicious that certain foods might be causing her son's symptoms, she began to monitor his diet. He ate more ice cream on the weekends than at any other time. She concluded that he might be sensitive to dairy products. She was then able to make adjustments to his diet. Her suspicions were confirmed.

The same woman's husband had suffered with bronchitis for years. By experimenting with different foods, she found that he was sensitive to gluten, which is found in baked goods. Then their youngest boy began to have all kinds of stomach problems, which she traced to foods made with yeast.

"It's a bit tough making meals for my family," she said, "but it's worth it. Everyone is healthier than ever before. We have a much happier family now."

Food Sensitivities

A woman wrote that she had long suffered with unexplained poor health. She got hives, she had difficulty breathing, and parts of her body swelled out of proportion. Furthermore, she had an irregular heartbeat, frazzled nerves, poor digestion, fatigue, and weakness.

This woman read in one of the ECK books the story of my visit to a nutritionist. This seemed like a good idea to her. She found one she liked, and after interviewing the woman, the nutritionist referred her to an applied kinesthesiologist. "He'll do muscle testing to find out which foods are good or bad for you."

The kinesthesiologist performed the appropriate tests, determined which foods he felt were harmful to her, and recommended certain changes in her diet. Soon after, all the problems—the hives, breathing difficulty, swelling, and so on—went away. She has been clear of symptoms for a year.

Different Kinds of Healing

Not so many years ago a person who delved into things such as muscle testing would have been considered a practitioner of black magic. That's how people were. But the consciousness has come far in the last few years. We now recognize there are different methods of healing, and one of these is to test for food allergies.

Eating the right kind of foods may not take care of all your problems. When a health condition keeps you from enjoying life as much as you should, you have to go to the proper health professional.

Often, though, people get so used to certain problems that they just figure that's the way it is. But if the discomfort interferes with one's work—such as a dentist whose hands hurt and don't function as they should—then it can be disastrous not to seek professional help.

I'm not a doctor, of course, so I can't prescribe anything for others. What I can do is share my own experiences with foods. One thing I've found is that some of us never quite learn the lesson about the effects of our diet.

During seminars I eat all my meals in restaurants. This makes it easy to get away from the healthy routines established at home, where you get into the habit of preparing foods that are good for you.

Salad Bar Story

The other day I went to a buffet. The salad bar had all the usual vegetables, but I wasn't in the mood for any of them. Then I spotted green olives and black olives. I filled a little plate with both kinds and helped myself to some of the other food.

As soon as I sat down at the table, I proceeded to eat every one of the olives. "These are really good," I said. So good, in fact, that I went back and filled another plate. By the time I finished the second helping, they didn't taste quite as good as when I'd started.

About two or three hours later I had an aching in the front of my head. "Why do I have this headache?" I asked myself. All of a sudden it popped into my mind: salt. Olives are prepared in salt; they're loaded with it. I had no choice but to wait it out until the headache ran its course.

Sweets

At the end of another meal, the waiter came over to take our orders for dessert. Others at the table ordered cheesecake, and I decided to have some too.

The waiter brought beautiful creamy wedges of cheese-cake. But when I looked at my piece I kept seeing chunks of cheese piled on a piece of crust. The strange image was my body's way of saying, "You don't really want this." But there it was in front of me, and my parents had taught me to clean my plate.

The headache came a few hours later, this time in the back of my head. "What is giving me this headache?" I wondered.

Even before I got through the question, the image came back: chunks of cheese on crust. It was the cheesecake.

Too Much of a Good Thing

The real problem wasn't the food; it was the fact that I ate too much of it. The next time we went back to the place where I'd eaten too many olives, I only took a few, and I was fine.

Sometimes even a good food can be a poison if you eat too much of it. There is really no food that is all good or all bad for everyone in general. Your reaction to a particular food will depend on your health conditions and on how much or how often you eat that food. Who knows better than you how you feel and what's right for you? This puts a lot of power in your hands.

Self-Image

Recently I talked with a person I have known for years. I almost didn't recognize him. At 178 pounds, he's half the man he used to be. The willpower it took to lose 180 pounds makes him twice the man he used to be. He carries himself well and looks very good. Now, of course, he has to deal with the issue of his self-image.

When you are anything other than average in body size, whether thin or ample, people often react to you in accordance with their own ideas about such things. The way they treat you tends to create within you a certain image of yourself.

This man had exercised an enormous amount of self-discipline to get to his new size, and it's going to take a lot more for him to stay there. Accustomed to being treated as a heavy person, he now has to get used to being perceived— and perceiving himself—as a slender person with a healthy body. This may require a real adjustment in his thinking.

Two Steps to Co-workership

In ECK we want to become a Co-worker with God. Basically there are two steps to co-workership. The first is to become a Co-worker with the Mahanta. This is like an apprenticeship. Once we have learned to let the ECK work through us all the time, we then become a Co-worker with God.

One is not less than the other. It's a transition; it doesn't just happen. The person who is learning to become a co-worker with life gives divine love back to life. He has learned to be grateful for the blessings that come to him. If you in ECK can learn to be grateful for the things that the Holy Spirit brings to you every day, you will have gained something that many other people have not found.

State Fair

Earlier this year I went to the Minnesota state fair, an event I enjoy because of all the people. It's one of the largest state fairs in the country.

As I wandered through the crowds, it was often shoulder to shoulder. Smoke from the hot-food stands swept across the crowds like the smoke on a battlefield. Children were running around; their parents, grandparents, and everybody else was eating and having a good time. A state fair offers a good opportunity for people to mingle and enjoy themselves, like a big family reunion.

I took a walk to the area where the farm machinery was displayed. In the twenty years since I left the farm, a lot of changes have taken place in farming. Tractor wheels now stand higher than my head.

A lot of changes have taken place in ECKANKAR too. I thought about these things as I walked among the swarms of people, realizing that I was there as a Co-worker.

One of the exhibits was a huge green farming machine. The family walking in front of me stopped to look at it. There were quite a few of them—parents, children, aunts, and uncles—all enjoying a reunion at the state fair.

A young man, about fifteen years old, asked his mother, "Hey, Mom, what's this green thing?"

"Ask your father," she said. "He grew up on a farm." Her voice was filled with pride.

The father strutted at the head of the group, like a scout leading the hunting party. Important as he tried to look, I was pretty sure he'd been off the farm at least as long as I had.

"Hey, Dad, what's this green machine?" the teenager asked.

"It's used for corn," said Dad.

"But what does it do?"

Dad was on the spot now. He had grown up on the farm and there was no way he would admit that he didn't know. "It's used for corn!" he repeated, in an even more commanding voice.

The father didn't know if it was used for picking corn, shredding corn, or popping corn. But the son knew it was a good time to let his question drop.

Changes

I had no idea what half these machines were for, either. Things really have changed.

The same sentiment has been shared by some people who left ECKANKAR for five or ten years and then came back. As they tried to get into the mainstream of ECKANKAR again, they could feel that something was different.

"Nothing is ever the same as it was before," I told them. This came as a surprise to some, but it's true. So much has happened since Paul Twitchell brought out the teachings of ECK twenty-five years ago. I left the farm

37

five or six years after that, and the changes kept coming—for ECKANKAR and for me.

In another twenty-five years, many of you will look back at 1990 and say, "Boy, those were the primitive, simple days when we celebrated the twenty-fifth anniversary of ECK. I remember it well. There was food, dancing, everybody having a good time. Those were the good old days of ECKANKAR."

Yellow Marigolds

Wherever we go, we are being a channel for God. The growing season was about over, but I wanted to buy some flowers to put around my yard. I drove to a nursery to see if they had any left. The parking lot was empty. I wondered if I would even be able to find a flower.

The greenhouse had a sliding door that led to the huge area where customers come in early spring to pick out their selection of marigolds, petunias, and geraniums.

Passing through the front part of the store to get to the greenhouse, I saw a few checkout counters but only one clerk and no other customers. I started to slide open the greenhouse door.

"Customers are not allowed back in the greenhouse area!" the clerk snapped. Her tone was abrupt and rude.

Whoa! I thought. I'm a peace-loving person who just wants a few flowers—I didn't come here for a fight. I quickly slid the door shut.

Behind the checkout counters were some leftover flowers that hadn't sold during the season. I debated whether or not to go look at them or just to get out of there.

Suddenly there was a commotion at the front of the store. A man angrily slammed a potted tree on the pave-

38

ment outside the door and came inside. Muttering curses, he stomped over to the counter. "I want a replacement or my money back!" he demanded. He looked quite upset.

The clerk, who obviously had her own problems, was not very cooperative. "We don't give returns," she said firmly. "We don't know what kind of care you gave to that tree since you bought it."

They stood there jaw to jaw, glaring at each other. Looks like it might turn into a fistfight, I thought. If I were a betting man, I'm not sure which one I'd put my money on.

Mentally I flipped a coin. Probably the man would win, I concluded. He's bigger, and besides that, he's madder.

But I wasn't there to get in the middle of a cat-and-dog fight. An incident like that can spoil an otherwise perfectly good day. With no intention of interfering in their experience, I decided to chant HU, a holy name for God.

Quietly, inside myself, I began to sing HU-U-U-U.

The rude clerk must have realized she was about to get a bloody nose. "I'm going to get my supervisor," she said, giving herself an honorable retreat.

Turning a Situation Around

The clerk took off for the back room and emerged immediately with a much younger woman who seemed quite calm. "What can I do for you?" the supervisor asked the angry customer.

"I bought this plant here, and it died!" he said.

"I'm sure we can work something out," she reassured him. "Let's go look at the tree."

Once outside, the supervisor quickly conceded that the tree was really dead. "It happens sometimes," she said.

"But the season is at an end and the trees are all sold out. We just don't have any more."

She paused for a moment, thinking of a way to appease the customer. Then she said, "I do have some hanging plants that come in several different price ranges. If you're interested, you can have your choice—even the most expensive one."

I waited for the customer's angry refusal. Instead he smiled and said, "That sounds pretty good to me."

The rude clerk, unhappy to see the matter resolved so smoothly, had to get in one final jab. "*You* let that tree die," she said.

"Shut up or I'm going to hit you!" he yelled. His expression left little doubt that he meant it.

The woman wasn't completely stupid. She must have realized she was lucky to still have her teeth. Meek as a lamb, she turned and went back to the checkout counter.

The man chose a hanging plant, and on his way to the door he had a few choice words for the clerk. But he did remember to thank the supervisor before he left.

Spiritual Giving

I went over to the checkout counter to ask the clerk a question. She was actually shaking. A violently angry customer is not an everyday occurrence.

"Can I help you find something?" she asked. She was very subdued now.

"I'm looking for yellow marigolds," I said. "All I see here are the bronze. I need the yellow ones to fill in some plants . . . " and here I said those delicate words, "that died at home." Then I hastily added, "But it wasn't your fault." I didn't want to set her off again.

40

"We have some more marigolds back here," she said. "They're closer to yellow than bronze. Maybe some of those would work?"

I went to look at them. She was right. "This one would work," I said. "And I notice that you have hanging plants. One of those would look quite nice in front of our home." I hadn't even thought of them until her argument with the customer.

"That man's anger was totally uncalled for," she said.

"Oh, yes," I said, giving her a very sympathetic look.

The clerk showed me several hanging plants, and I picked out the one I liked. Then she told me the price. "Oh, my goodness," I said. "That's pretty expensive. I thought it was the same price as the first few you showed me."

"That's OK," she said. "I'll let you have it for the price of the cheaper ones."

This was her gift to me for showing sympathy. But she wasn't finished giving. On top of a nice discount on the hanging plant, she threw in the marigolds for free.

The clerk probably didn't realize that she was involved in spiritual giving. All she'll remember about that day is the angry customer who came in and acted totally unreasonable.

But our reaction to an experience like this depends on our state of consciousness. These things go on all the time. It's not what happens in our daily life, it's the state of consciousness we carry with us that makes our life heaven or hell.

Video Tokens

There is never a charge for an initiation in ECK. The individual brings a gift of fruit or flowers for God, which is accepted by the ECK Initiator.

Around the time of the dedication of the Temple of ECK, I accepted the gift of fruit from an individual who had just gotten his initiation. Then he said, "Here are four tokens to use at a video arcade. These are for you personally."

Occasionally someone tries to send me money out of gratitude for their initiation. The money is a gift to God, so I just give it to ECKANKAR as a donation.

But these tokens were nonrefundable. I couldn't take them to the video arcade and redeem them for a dollar bill to send to ECKANKAR.

When I got home, I stuck the tokens in the watch pocket of my jeans, figuring I could decide later what to do with them. There happened to be one more token in my pocket, so now I had five. Then I forgot all about them.

When I write, the spiritual energy from the ECK comes through so strongly that I have to do something to get rid of it. A visit to a video arcade diffuses the ECK flow more quickly than anywhere else I can go. Plus I enjoy being with people.

After I got home from the dedication on Monday, the spiritual energy was strong. "I'm going to check the mail and run some errands," I told my wife. A trip to the video arcade was not on my list.

Short of cash, I drove to a store that had an automatic teller machine. "We don't have the ATM anymore," a clerk informed me. "Management took it out when we remodeled."

I wasn't very familiar with that part of town, so I drove down the street with an eye out for another ATM. About a block from the store was a video arcade. I suppose I could go there, I thought. The energy I was trying to burn off was still strong.

Reaching into my pocket, I discovered the tokens that the ECKist had given me. I inserted one in a machine and really got absorbed in the game. Then I went over to Ms. Pac-Man. A young man had the machine tied up, so I played a few other games while waiting for him to finish.

All of a sudden I spotted three people, a mother and her two children, with their spiritual lights on. I knew they were ECKists. I can always pick them out of a crowd, whether they look my way or not. The spiritual Light of ECK comes through them very strongly.

All three were looking my way, beaming and smiling. I went over and we exchanged greetings. "Were you at the dedication today?" I asked the mother.

"No, we weren't," she said. She then went on to explain why they happened to be at the video arcade on a school day. That morning her son and daughter had pointed out that Monday, October 22, was the ECK new year. "But we never get a day off from school to celebrate it."

The mother wanted to be fair. "OK," she said, "I'll call the school, and we'll all take a day off and spend it together."

This particular video arcade gives a free token for each A on a child's report card. Both of her children were A students. They had cashed in the A's for tokens, and by the time I came over to say hello, the son was on the Star Wars machine. I was watching him play when all of a sudden the young man finished with Ms. Pac-Man and the machine was open. "Quick," I said to the mother. "Ms. Pac-Man is open, but you've got to move fast in here."

"I gave my last token to my son," she said. I was out of tokens too. I had used up the four given to me by the ECKist and had given her son the fifth one to play another Star Wars game.

"I'll go get you some," I offered.

"No, no, no," she protested.

"It's no big deal. I'll go get them." I put my dollar in the machine for four tokens, then handed them to the mother.

Suddenly I realized what was happening: This was the dollar's worth of tokens that the ECKist had given to me at his initiation. I had used them, but now I was giving them back.

Ice-Cream Bar

We had a very enjoyable time, then left the arcade together and said our farewells. Before I ran into them I had begun to feel tired and drained from the long day. But now I felt refreshed. When I meet ECKists, the ECK current flows strongly through me and the tiredness goes away.

"You need an ice-cream bar," I said to myself. "You deserve the best today."

I got in my car and drove to a shopping mall in what I thought was a remote part of town. By now it was dark outside. Seeing a snack shop, I parked and got out of the car. I had barely slammed the door shut when another car pulled up. In it were three people—oh, no!—with their spiritual lights on.

Good heavens, I thought. More ECKists. But maybe it's for the best: I can't go in that store and buy an ice-cream bar now; they'll see me. I have to set a good example.

Inside I went to the cooler and got myself a bottle of water. Then I quickly paid the clerk and left. The whole transaction probably took about half a minute.

The three ECKists had just gotten out of their car. As

it turned out, they weren't coming into the same store at all. They were going to the Chinese restaurant right next door.

Up close I recognized them as three Higher Initiates that I wanted to talk with. They had come to Minneapolis for the dedication of the Temple of ECK, but with so many other people around, we hadn't been able to meet. The ECK had brought us together out here. If our timing had been off by even ten seconds, we would have missed each other.

"We wondered why there were so many delays as we were trying to get out to dinner tonight," one of them said.

"This is how the ECK works," I said—and tried not to think about the ice-cream bar.

There were a few things I wanted to discuss with one of the Higher Initiates. He had gone through some very hard times of late. He had been job-hunting for months, and I was concerned about how he was doing. Recently I had written him with some recommendations, and he wrote back to say that he had already tried everything. A day or two after sending his letter, he landed a position with a very good company.

A onetime resident of Minnesota, he knew about the Chinese restaurant in this isolated shopping mall. That's why he and the two other ECKists happened to be here.

"Have you gotten your first paycheck yet?" I asked him.

"Not yet," he answered.

"Then," one of the women said, "dinner's on us." That was a very nice touch. The ECK works from end to end, time and again.

With errands still to do, I went to another store. There I happened to find the brand of ice-cream bar that I can eat occasionally, so I bought it. It was delicious. Under the circumstances, I considered it a health food. It was good for me because I needed the emotional boost.

Light and Joy

The light and joy that you find in your own life is always from the ECK. In ECKANKAR you learn to come into a conscious awareness of how the Holy Spirit works for you in everything you do. And seeing this, you become filled with more love and goodness.

ECK Worldwide Seminar, Orlando, Florida,
Sunday, October 28, 1990

Soon people began to stop by just to say, "Your flowers are so pretty." She didn't realize it yet, but this was the help she had requested: God was using her garden to break down the wall between her and the neighbors.

5

God's Help in Every Trouble

A couple I met during my last trip to Australia were expecting a baby. They were also building a new home. On this visit they told me the baby is growing up and the home is nearly finished.

The husband showed me photographs of the house, a well-designed structure with some very advanced features. I was reminded of an interview I'd heard on a radio talk show. The guest was a man who had built his own home and written a book about it. At the end of the program the host asked, "Do you have a word of advice for those in the audience who would like to build their own home?"

"Yes," said the guest. "Don't do it."

How to Take the Next Step

When I saw the ECKist who had built his own home, I asked him, "If you had it to do over again, would you still build your home from the bottom up?"

"Never," he said.

He's an inventive person who comes up with solutions easily. But he still ran up against a brick wall more than once. "There were times when I just didn't know what to do or how to take the next step," he said.

But he also found that whenever he reached that point, help would appear. Someone unexpected would turn up. "It was always exactly the right person who could solve the problem," he added. "Often this person could do the work for a fraction of what it would have normally cost." Even in something like building his own home, this ECK chela noticed that God's help came when and where he least expected it.

Changed Attitude

The purpose of the ECK teachings is not just to have experiences of God's help, but to learn to recognize them when they come. This is consciousness—being aware of what is happening in your life.

An interesting article in *Reader's Digest* was written by a Catholic woman. In her younger years, most of her time had been spent tripping over little problems. She felt that if she could somehow get past these little problems, she would be able to get on with her life.

One day it finally dawned on her: These little problems *were* her life. From the moment she recognized and accepted that fact, her whole attitude toward living changed. Life became a challenge in which the so-called stumbling blocks were actually opportunities for her spiritual growth.

Banana Peels

When these problems come up in your life, how do you handle them? Do you stumble and fall? Or do you just trip a little and then take a running half step to keep from falling all the way down?

A certain woman has the bad habit of criticizing people. She doesn't understand that her criticism of others is the cause of so many of her own problems. Over and over she slips, falls, and hurts herself, unaware that she is slipping and falling spiritually.

As we walk along through life, occasionally we step on a banana peel, and down we go. But after this happens three, four, or five times, most of us catch on. Then we say, "OK, the next time I see a banana peel, I'm going to walk around it."

Sometimes it's much easier to see another person's banana peel. How could he miss it? It's as big as a throw rug. When he slips on it anyway, we say, "Oh, my goodness, he must have the consciousness of a banana."

Our vision changes when it comes to our own problems, of course. The banana peels that trip us up are always microscopic in size, so how could we possibly have seen them? "Where did this come from? Somebody else must have put it there. I slipped only because so-and-so did this or that to me," we complain.

How God's Help Comes

As humans, we are actually quite amusing. We would see the humor if we just had the presence of mind to look at ourselves in a mirror.

A true mirror would show us that our banana peels are as big as anybody else's. If we saw someone slip and create a problem because of a spiritual oversight, we would know that this could be our banana peel too. Instead of criticizing, we would say, "If it happened to him, it could happen to me."

But people are funny. At the first sign of trouble, it's, "God, please help me in my hour of need." As if God had nothing better to do than to pick up after those who refuse to look out for their own banana peels. Maybe they think God's sole job is to pick them up, set them on their feet, watch them fall, pick them up, watch them fall, and pick them up again.

Sometimes the spiritual help comes through another person acting as a vehicle for God. But because it comes in the form of another human being, we may not recognize it as help from God. Still, even a person who is only half conscious will say thank you to the one who helped.

A less conscious person may say, "God, please help me." But if the help happens to come from someone of the wrong color, the wrong religion, the wrong political party, or whatever, he won't accept it. "I don't deal with your kind," he'll say, and turn the person away. Then he'll go right back to asking, "Oh, God, please help me." It never occurs to him that maybe God sent that particular person to help.

Horseradish

A woman wrote to advice columnist Ann Landers about an experience she had while having lunch at a restaurant with a friend. The letter writer, who apparently has a very good digestive system, ordered roast beef, potatoes, and horseradish. She was busy talking to her friend when she aimed her fork at what she thought were the potatoes. Unaware that it had landed in the horseradish, she scooped up a healthy forkful and stuffed it into her mouth.

The pungent taste caught her completely by surprise. She sucked in her breath, then tried to breathe out but couldn't. She began to sweat. Rising to her feet, she struggled to expel her breath as she motioned to her friend for help. But the other woman just stared at her in horror, too paralyzed to move.

A man seated on the far side of the restaurant saw what was happening. He jumped up, dashed across the room, and gave the choking woman a sharp slap on the back. Suddenly she could breathe again.

The man held on to her as she sat back down in her chair. "There, now, you'll be OK," he said soothingly. "You'll be all right." Then he went back to his table to finish his meal.

After saying a few prayers of thanksgiving, the woman went over to talk to her rescuer. "Thank you," she said, "you saved my life." He acknowledged her expression of gratitude with the kindest smile she had ever seen. Soon after that, he got up and left the restaurant.

During the minute and a half she had spent gasping for breath, the woman's thoughts had been focused on her children: What will happen to them? She probably also thought, "Please help me, God." Her own logical choice was the friend seated right across the table from her. But her friend was so frozen with fear that she was not able to be of any help.

Then, just in the nick of time, God sent somebody from the other side of the restaurant who knew the right thing to do. I can almost imagine God coming home that night and saying to Mrs. God, "This woman picked the wrong person to ask for help, but thank goodness she didn't fight off the right guy when he came over to help."

An experience like this is not always recognized as help from God, but that's what it was. People have a tendency to credit those who give the help, without realizing that behind it all is the divine power. On the other hand, some help probably does come more from another human being than from God; it just depends on what we were up to when we asked for it. God doesn't always grant our every request.

Giving God Credit

Two radio sports commentators were talking about the routine that many teams follow before a game. One of them said, "Each team prays to God to help them win. But did you ever hear the losing team give credit to God?"

That was a perceptive comment. If there is any mention of God from the team that lost, it's probably connected to a profanity.

Before the game it was total humility: "If it's God's will, we'll win." Afterward they're certain that if some stupid player hadn't dropped the ball at a critical time, they would have scored more points and won the game.

You would also expect the winning team to give credit to God after the game. Instead, they pay tribute to themselves: how smart they were, how well they planned the moves, how hard they practiced beforehand, and so on. Win or lose, you rarely hear another word about God's will.

Knowing What to Do

A few days ago my wife and I had left a restaurant and were walking back to our hotel. A group of Japanese tourists passed us on their way back to their tour bus. Just ahead of us was a family—an elderly couple, their two daughters who looked around thirty, and a few younger people. All of a sudden the old gentleman toppled forward in a swan dive, heading straight for the pavement.

"Look, he's falling," I said to my wife, and we rushed over to help. On the way down, the man reached out and caught hold of a low stone wall, no more than a foot high, that ran along the edge of the sidewalk. That move saved him from serious injury. Instead of landing face first on the pavement, he tipped and landed very neatly on his side. Then he rolled over on his stomach, unconscious.

One of the daughters tugged at her father, trying to get him up. As I helped her turn him over on his back, I noticed that he had sustained only a slight cut over his left eye. His chest moved up and down, so we knew he was breathing, and his lips stayed their normal color rather than turning blue.

Pretty soon he opened his eyes and looked around. Seeing that everyone around him was quite calm, he lay there quietly for a moment, then gave his daughter a weak smile.

A passerby came over and offered to call an ambulance. "No, wait," the daughter said. She couldn't speak English very well, but I could almost read her thoughts: how inconvenient it would be if the bus left without them, the cost of a visit to the hospital if he wasn't really hurt, and so on. So we waited.

A minute or two later the gentleman shook his head to clear it, then motioned with his hand that he was ready to get up. We helped him to a standing position. When he felt steady enough, he turned to me, bowed politely, and said something in Japanese. "He thanks you," his daughter translated.

"It's all right," I said. My wife and I stood and watched as the family members helped him back to the bus.

Sometimes we are put in a position to be a channel for help. My wife and I left the restaurant because we had finished our meal, yet there was another purpose for our being outside at that particular time.

When an unexpected situation like this comes up, you can't help wondering if you'll know what to do. It might surprise you to find that you do. As you deal with it to the best of your ability, you realize that you have a sense of knowing.

Where does this knowing come from? Those of you who accept reincarnation as a fact realize that you have gone through just about every experience that one could have. In another life, you may have ministered to others as a medic on the battlefield. And at some level you carry these memories with you. So when a sudden emergency comes up and you find that you know exactly what to do, you may be drawing on experiences from the past.

Purpose of Life

What is the purpose of life? is a big question for most people. In ECK we say it's to gain experience so that we can become a Co-worker with God.

When I was in Christianity, I wasn't quite sure why I was here on earth, except possibly to put in my time until I died. Then I would be put in a grave, lie there in darkness until the last day, and some time after that, be in paradise. That, I thought, was the sum total of my life. It seemed like such a waste of time.

Nor did it make sense that at the eleventh hour a person who had lived an entirely selfish life could beg for forgiveness and be released from all responsibility. According to that scenario, a person on his deathbed could call in a priest and be absolved of all sins. Then he would go straight to heaven, to be greeted by St. Peter and angels saying, "Hosanna, hosanna, here he comes. We knew what this old crook was up to the whole time. But he beat the odds—he made it in."

Apparently it didn't matter that he had lived his whole life with the destructive intent to rob and injure others. It was as if everything he had ever done in the past counted for nothing.

The whole idea struck me as a misunderstanding of some divine law. If for every action there is an equal and opposite reaction, and whatsoever a man soweth, that also shall he reap, then something didn't seem right.

Becoming a Co-worker with God

I'd always had the sense that the Law of Life was just. And it is just. At some point in our lives, our attitudes and actions come back to us, giving each of us the experiences that we have earned. The purpose of these experiences is to make us more conscious of why we are actually here. Gradually we learn that it's not just to tread water while we put in our time, it's to become a Co-worker with God.

But how do you become a Co-worker with God? It is not necessary to give up everything, leave your family, and go off to a monastery proclaiming, "I now devote my life to God!"

Monastic orders and celibacy were not part of the early Catholic church. These practices were adopted later, because some of the clergy felt more comfortable living single lives. This is perfectly all right, but to practice celibacy because you think it makes you more spiritual is wrong. It's a form of vanity that seeks to put one Soul above another.

This is not to say that everyone who belongs to a monastic order or practices celibacy has this feeling of vanity. Many of the people in these orders truly have the sense of being a Co-worker with God. In one way or another they have devoted their lives to the service of others. They realize that to serve any of God's creatures is to serve God.

On the other hand, a person can dress up in fine clothing, piously attend church every Sunday, make a big show of being ethical, and not be very spiritual. Who can say? Who can read the heart of another? Spirituality is not segregated according to any of the categories conceived by man, whether religion, race, political party, or economic status.

What Is Spirituality?

What, then, is spirituality built on? What makes a person spiritual? I say it's experience. The more experience a person has—including that from past lives—the more likely he is to be spiritual.

But experience by itself is not the quality that we see in a spiritual person. You can't look at someone and say, "Oh, you have a lot of experience of a spiritual kind." This is not really an observable quality.

You can, however, look at someone and see that he or she has a lot of compassion and love for others. That kind of love—divine love—is a spiritual quality. And where did that divine love come from? From experience.

In the teachings of ECK, we put a lot of stock in experiences with the Light and Sound of God. These are very important. But the experiences themselves mean nothing unless they bring you love.

What you are looking for is divine love. A spiritual path ought to transform you into a spiritual being who is filled with love. That should be the test of your religion.

Those Who Have Love

Some people spend their whole life in one religion simply because they were born into it. But they never find love. They don't even know what it means. Still, they may have loyalty and devotion to the religion, and this is a step. Eventually you find that all loyalty is built upon a loyalty to the divine principle, or God.

Will you always be loyal to God? That is what some people are getting from their religion in this lifetime. But they are not spiritually advanced enough to have love.

It's as if the world has a great big line drawn right down the center. On one side are those who have love, and on the other are those who do not. People who have love can recognize others who have it, while those who do not have it cannot recognize it. Furthermore, people who do not have love don't know that they don't have it.

How do you come to the state of being filled with love? You can't just know love; you have to be filled with love. This is probably the greatest gift of God you can ask for.

People who are ill often say, "God, please heal my illness," and this is OK. But you can also ask something that is beneficial for you spiritually, in a 360-degree type of way. You can say, "Dear God, teach me how to love."

If you ask this of the divine power with sincerity, with a desire to know truth, I can guarantee you that your life will change—in very dramatic ways. It won't necessarily start out that way, but eventually it will pick up speed.

So when you ask the Lord of Life, "Show me truth," be ready to receive it. You have to ask with a true and open heart, for only a person who is sincere can ask the question truly.

Behind everything that you do is the life pulse of the Holy Spirit, the Voice of God, which we call the ECK. The

Voice of God comes down and speaks to us as the Light and Sound. This is what fills one with divine love.

In your spiritual life you somehow have to learn how to come in contact with these two aspects of the Holy Spirit, the Light and Sound of God. The way to do it is through singing the word HU, a love song to God. If you ask God for divine love and you ask sincerely, you will be opened up to divine love.

Opening the Heart

As I give these talks, sometimes I notice that individuals in the audience are not receptive. Everything went wrong as they tried to get to the ECK seminar—the car broke down, the flight was delayed. By the time they finally arrive, they're exhausted from all the problems.

They may not realize it, but along the way they got a lot of experience. The Holy Spirit softened them up so that they would be a little more able to accept some of the things they heard about truth.

Often I start by telling stories because they open the heart. Only when the hearts are opened can I begin to speak more direct truth. If I sense that the audience as a group is tightened in consciousness, I continue to talk in stories and parables.

The New Testament is a fascinating testament that has been misunderstood by so many people. Christ once told his closest disciples that while he spoke in parables to the multitudes, to them he spoke the truth. He was drawing a distinction between the consciousness of his disciples and that of the general audiences.

Indeed, most of the words attributed to Christ in the New Testament are in parable form. It's as if the secret teachings were never recorded. Sent by God to bring truth to people, he spoke it and demonstrated it in the things he did. Sometimes people recognized it, but I think the writers of the New Testament were more enthralled by the miracles.

It's the same today. If somebody were to perform a miracle, that would make news. Like a good story, it's easy to put down in writing. But to distill a spiritual truth and bring it out in simple terms is very difficult. Some of the most beautiful writings in the New Testament are the beatitudes, where the truth was given very directly.

Recognizing Truth

If you are open to the Holy Spirit, you will find truth coming to you through the actions and words of other people. This is a facet of the ECK-Vidya, the ancient science of prophecy. I call it the Golden-tongued Wisdom.

When God speaks to you through others, the words may even come via the electronic media. For instance, the radio or TV is on. Suddenly a sentence pops out that is precisely for you. It may mean nothing to anyone else, but for you it has a significant meaning.

This is just one of the ways God speaks to you. If you are aware enough to notice it when it happens, you will find that it is always a constructive, positive kind of a statement. It builds; it's never destructive. If a destructive statement ever pops out, there is no need to wonder, Is this a message from God to help me spiritually? Of course not. It has to be uplifting; it has to be for the good of creation, for the good of mankind. Anything destructive is never for your spiritual good.

Living a Life of Truth

In every religion you will find people who take advantage of others in their own group. Even among ECKists there are those who would use the teachings of ECK to influence other members. One example involves healings. There are ECKists who are in licensed fields of healing. If another ECKist comes to them for that purpose, this is fine; it's what the practitioner is trained and licensed to do.

On the other hand, some practitioners are not licensed but are selling health services or products, and his or her business is based completely on ECKists. Then I have to ask, "How true can that healing system be if the person can only make a living from other ECKists?"

A friend's son is a Mormon missionary here in Australia. As in any other group, he has found that the crooks among the Mormons will prey upon the other members, sometimes almost viciously. There is nothing wrong with Mormons doing business with each other, but when one sets out to cheat the devout and trusting members of their group, that is wrong.

In ECK, too, there is nothing wrong with people helping each other through their professions. But it should never be done by cheating. For instance, if one ECKist tells another, "Here is a technique that can help you, but you have to be cleared through this or that other teaching," that is wrong. The ECK teachings are not based on removing karma through clearing by other masters.

If anyone ever says something to you along this line, or implies that I have put my stamp of approval on such things that are not of the ECK teachings, tell them, "This is wrong. Go somewhere else, please." Let them prey on their own people, whoever they are. They're certainly not the ECKists.

The people who are doing this sort of thing have to decide whether or not they really want to be members of

ECK. We must be honest with each other in our dealings. It's wrong to try to pawn off our livelihood on others through dishonesty. The same applies no matter what group you're in.

Pushy

A couple in England moved to a retirement bungalow. The wife, an ECKist, is a very outgoing person. She couldn't wait to make friends with everyone in their new community. When the neighbors came by to visit, she was so happy to meet them. She greeted each person who walked past her home and engaged them in conversation.

Pretty soon she noticed that the neighbors were snubbing her. Not only did they stop coming by, they actually began to ignore her. When they saw her outside, they would hurry by before she could speak to them.

At first she couldn't figure out why no one wanted to be friendly. Then one day it dawned on her: Though she was a happy person who liked to talk to everyone, the neighbors thought she was pushy. That's why they were avoiding her.

The situation really saddened her because she had a strong need to be with people. But since the neighbors misunderstood her intentions, she decided that the only thing she could do was just let it be. Finally she turned it over to the ECK, the Holy Spirit, saying, "I need help on this. I don't know what to do."

Human beings have a need for other people; it's just that simple. We have a sense of community. In Christianity the people like to come together in a group on Sundays. ECKists like to get together, too, which is one of the purposes of the ECK seminars. They are a way to fulfill our sense of community and to grow. We gather together to learn from each other and see how the Holy Spirit works through us and through others, back and forth. The interaction helps uplift us spiritually.

Ways to Give Love

With no one to talk to, the ECKist turned her attention to her new home. The lawn and garden had been neglected before they bought the property, so she and her husband decided to do something about it. First they got out the lawn mower and mowed the lawn. They fashioned a nice, rounded border for the garden. Then they turned up the earth and put in compost and fertilizer. Once the soil was prepared, they went to a greenhouse and bought some shrubs, flowers, and bulbs.

The woman devoted herself to gardening. She had tried to give her love to her neighbors but they wouldn't accept it. She had to give love somewhere, so she put it all into creating the most beautiful garden.

Soon people began to stop by just to say, "Your flowers are so pretty. Your shrubs look so good. It all blends together so well." She didn't realize it yet, but this was the help she had requested: God was using her garden to break down the wall between her and the neighbors.

"For now we speak only about the garden," she told me, "but someday we'll go on to other things. They'll start to ask me questions about myself, and then we'll talk about ECK."

This experience showed her that people need time to accept things at their own pace. We don't want to be pushed, so we shouldn't push others. We have an understanding of how the Holy Spirit works, but so do others. We feel that our spiritual path is right; others feel the same about theirs. If our path helps us spiritually, then maybe theirs does the same for them. So just let them be. If you want to do something, just love them for who they are and let it be.

Pretty soon they'll notice that you have a quality they haven't seen very often, and they'll be curious to know where you got this love. They might start by commenting on the flowers in your garden. Then they'll want to talk to you about other things, such as an illness in their family.

Whenever they want to talk, all you have to do is be there. Gradually you'll learn about them, and they'll learn about you. In the process you're going to be raised spiritually, but so will they. This is another of the laws of life: As one person is raised spiritually, so are all others.

A Spiritual Need to Fill

The churches in Europe have noticed a drop in attendance. In America, though many people still go to church on Sundays, some of the mainline denominations have also lost followers. The leaders are recognizing that their churches are in trouble. They are trying to find out why people are leaving.

Those who are leaving have a spiritual need: they want truth, they want spiritual food. They are not finding it in their churches. Many are upset because the churches are so involved in social and political causes.

Church leadership may have forgotten what the people need, but the people haven't forgotten. And now they're looking for it elsewhere.

In this Year of the Vahana, the ECK missionary, we have to learn how to speak about ECK in everyday terms to people who want to know about God and divine love. This will be our challenge, not only in the coming year but in the coming decade. We have a big job ahead.

Many people are waiting for the message of ECK, because they too want to go home to God.

*South Pacific Regional Seminar, Adelaide, Australia,
Saturday, December 1, 1990*

Since it was her mother's decision, the daughter had to let her make up her own mind. She did nothing except sit there and love her mother.

6

Dear God, Use Me as You Will

Sometimes this world and the inner worlds are pretty much the same for me. Before you start out on the path of ECK and for a while after, the dream world is a mixed-up jumble of images that don't make much sense.

Then, as you go along in ECK, there are times when the dream world seems to stop completely, and you don't remember anything. At that point you wonder, "What's happening to my spiritual unfoldment? Has it stopped?"

It hasn't stopped. The Dream Master is allowing you to have the experiences without being burdened out here with the memory of them.

Expectations

People start out with certain expectations about the dream worlds and heaven. If you were to have an inner experience that showed you the true nature of the other worlds before you were ready, you might feel the truth was too much to take. This could put you into a state of imbalance. The Dream Master often pulls down the curtain to spare you from having to make such mental adjustments.

The mind will always try to turn the inner experience into something nice and neat. If you learned too suddenly how the other worlds are run, you'd probably find that it's not the way you expected it to be. "Heaven can't be this way!" you'd say.

Without having any experience, most people still have very strong ideas about what heaven should or should not be. To have opinions on things we know nothing about is a natural inclination of the human race.

Vahana Dreams

Those of you who have been in ECK for several years occasionally have a dream in which someone asks you about ECK. You may not remember the details of the experience or the name of the individual you met. But you know that the Holy Spirit was using you to reach someone with the message of ECK. You know that you were a vehicle for the Light and Sound of God in the dream state.

Sometimes the people you meet in the dream state live entirely on the inner planes. The dream state applies only in the lower worlds—the Astral, Causal, Mental, and Etheric Planes—but not beyond. They end just short of the Soul Plane, which is the Fifth Plane. This is the first of the worlds of true Spirit.

Other times you may recognize someone who lives here on earth. It may be a person you have met. It may be someone you've seen around but never have gotten to know in your outer life. When you wake up and remember the dream of talking with this person, you may wonder, "Was this a true experience?" Yes, it was a true experience. You were aware of that person, and he or she was aware of you—but only through the dream state.

For a while you may fluctuate between these periods of remembrance and forgetfulness. But as you go further in ECK, the periods of forgetfulness become less frequent. You begin to remember more and more about what you are doing on the other planes. You also find that these other worlds are divided into many different areas.

More than One Heaven

Growing up in Christianity, I was taught to think in terms of one heaven. We had no idea what was there, what the people did there, or anything else. In ECK we learn that there are many different levels to heaven.

Some of the people at the first level of heaven, just beyond earth, are looking for truth too. It might seem like a strange concept that anyone in heaven would be looking for truth. But in the lower regions of heaven, some—not all—are doing just that.

We find the same thing here on earth: Not everyone is looking for truth, but some people are. The rest are busy gaining their experiences in one way or another. They follow the path of ambition, striving to reach great heights in the corporate world. Or they put their energy into trying to find romance or something else.

They don't yet realize that if they would open up to the spiritual truths, all the different elements of their life would come together and take on a whole new light. Life would become much more interesting than before.

An Interesting Life

Life does become more interesting in ECK. We don't necessarily gain materialistically or acquire more goods.

We simply become more conscious of what is happening in our world.

There is something to be said for awareness, for knowing. Knowledge is very comforting to some people. For instance, if you're driving to an ECK seminar and the car breaks down in some remote area between cities, you feel fortunate if you know how to fix it. Even if you can only get the car to the next gas station, you've gotten yourself out of a tight spot. Being able to help yourself gives you a certain sense of satisfaction.

This is also true in the spiritual life. As we unfold spiritually, we get a deep sense of satisfaction. The more we understand how the laws of the Holy Spirit work, the more comfortable we are with life.

When the ups and downs do come, the first little ripple doesn't knock us to the ground and leave us there for too long. We are able to say, "OK, that was a blip on the radar screen of life." We say, "This too shall pass."

Longing for Truth

About a year ago I met a very nice gentleman on the inner planes. I mentioned ECK briefly, but mostly we talked on general subjects. He was the owner of a restaurant.

Yes, people on the other planes do eat, though you may have heard that it's not necessary on the Astral Plane. On the very low Astral Plane they don't eat food directly as we do here. They consume it vicariously, through the appetites of those on earth who are into gluttony, drinking, and some of the other passions of life.

Though the people on the lower Astral Plane do not need to take in food as we do, those on the higher Astral Plane do eat. It's different once you get to the very highest planes, of course. There, in the true spiritual worlds, the

Soul Plane and above, Soul subsists on the Light and Sound of God.

Recently I went back to this same city on the inner planes. My wife and I were walking along the street with two other people when the restaurant owner saw us. He came out to say hello.

"Come in," he said. "I'd like to talk with you. I'll go get a table ready for you." He ran back inside without waiting to see whether or not we could stay. As it turned out, we had an appointment in another place very soon.

Through the doorway I saw him clear a table for us. Then he came back out and said, "Please come in." I explained our situation and noticed his look of disappointment. "But if you have a question, you can ask it now," I said. "I may not be back in town for another year or so."

"I want to know about ECK," he said. "You talked about it last time, and I want to become a member."

I was a bit taken aback by this. Before I could respond, one of the people in my party said, "I'll be going to the ECK Center in this area within eighteen hours, and I'll send you some material. If you still want to become a member of ECK, you'll have whatever you need."

The longing for truth in this man's eyes was so strong. A person like this, who wants to find the teachings of ECK, is the kind of person I want to find. In this Year of the Vahana, the ECK missionary, I am asking the ECKists to help me find those who really want to know truth. And they are going to come along quite unexpectedly.

Light of Love

One individual found out about ECK in a very interesting way. Her roommate, an interior decorator, was at the home of a client. During a lull in activity, she began

73

chatting with the young son of the couple for whom she was decorating. She didn't know it, of course, but they were an ECK family.

Suddenly the boy said to her, "Do you like to read?"

"Sure," she answered. "I like books."

"I've got some good books upstairs," he said. "I'd like to give you one."

Assured that he had his mother's approval, she accepted his gift of an ECK book. Though she had never heard of ECKANKAR before, she accepted it politely and took it home.

That night she showed it to her roommate, and the two of them read it from cover to cover. Right after that the decorator saw an announcement about a showing of an ECK video on dreams. She found the place and time it would be shown. Though she had other plans that day, she mentioned it to her roommate, who decided to go.

This curious chain of events seemed to line up in a very natural way. It started when a young boy was able to recognize the light of love in another person—the interior decorator. This shining light was a love for truth. He was moved to give her something that was very precious to him—an ECK book. The decorator then saw a notice about the ECK dream video. Unable to attend the showing herself, she told her roommate about it. The roommate came. And so, by this very indirect route, someone found the teachings of ECK.

The modern-day ECK teachings were brought out in 1965. Although ECKANKAR is actually quite a young religion, we have members around the world, in Europe, Australia, North and South America, Africa, and Asia.

The Nature of Truth

An ECKist in Switzerland had been very ill. When she recovered, she realized that the only reason for living was to serve God. Of course, like most of us, she was faced with the fact that she had to go to work every day to make a living, but this is part of serving God.

It's not by accident that many of us have to work for a living. Some people think if they could win the lottery, they'd be spared from this plight. They think they could then get on with their life and really serve God.

Lotteries are quite popular in the United States. It's funny how it works. Let the politicians raise the taxes, and there's a revolt; let them bring in the lottery, and people willingly hand over their last dime. The politicians get the money one way or another, but as long as there's a chance to get something back, the people don't seem to mind.

One day the woman in Switzerland was about to leave work and go out for lunch. Basically she's a happy person, but on that particular day she felt down.

"I don't like being in a blue mood," she thought. "I have to get myself on the brighter side of life. I'm going to change my attitude and go to lunch with a good feeling."

Before she left for the restaurant, she had a quiet talk with the Mahanta. This is the word for the Inner Master, the high spiritual consciousness in ECKANKAR. It is akin to what is known in Christianity as the Christ consciousness. "Please, Mahanta," she said, "let me be a vehicle for you."

At the restaurant she was seated across from a gentleman who enjoyed talking. "I'm seventy-six years old," he informed her. "I'm originally from Austria but now I live in New York. I've lived there for years. Have you ever been to the States?"

"Yes, I have," she said. "I go there for ECKANKAR seminars."

The man asked about the ECK seminars. From there they got on the subject of how Divine Spirit works and some of the laws of life. He brought up questions which she was able to answer from her studies in ECK.

As they talked, she could see a light coming into his eyes. He began to speak with eagerness. "This is what I've been looking for," he said. Then he added, "No one can do it for us—we must do it for ourselves."

The man realized that although truth is always there, always available, we have to recognize it and take it for ourselves. No one can push truth on us. People often try to force their religion on others, but when it's done that way, it doesn't come in the nature of truth.

In ECK we work very hard at not imposing our teachings on others. Even though it may be truth, by the mere act of pushing it, you lose the nature of truth in it. Therefore, the person on the receiving end can't accept it as truth.

The gentleman wanted to find out more about ECK, so the woman gave him the address of some ECKists in New York, as well as the ECKANKAR Spiritual Center in Minneapolis. By then it was time for her to go back to work.

Later she thought about what had occurred. She'd started the day in a blue mood. Before leaving for lunch, she had asked to be of service to God. By the time she got to the restaurant, the opportunity was there.

The woman was able to have her lunch, be of service to the ECK, then get back to work on time and in a much better mood. This is a marvelous example of how the Holy

Spirit operates, following the Law of Economy, to make everything work out right.

Being Used as a Vehicle

No matter how carefully they test the sound system at the seminars, as soon as I get to the microphone, it often stops working the way it should. Furthermore, during a recent airplane trip, the overhead bulbs in our row began to put on their own peculiar little light show, flashing on and off at will, doing whatever they pleased. They refused to be controlled by the light switch in the armrest.

Those of you who have been in ECK a while may have noticed similar incidents. When the Holy Spirit is using you as a vehicle, things happen around you. It's not that you're causing them, or that you want them to happen, or that you're playing with the forces of nature to affect the natural course of events. To do that is to dabble in black magic.

Some people bend the forces of nature to "help" people— and I purposely put the word *help* in quotes. They dabble in what is called white magic. There is no point in dealing with these things.

To help someone in this way means that you have taken a load of karma from them before they were ready to have it removed naturally. Karma is removed naturally when the person is raised in spiritual awareness to the point where he realizes why he took it on in the first place. Once you recognize what you did in spiritual ignorance to cause yourself a certain problem, in many cases the karmic burden can begin to work itself off.

This is not always the case, of course. Sometimes we have to deal with lifelong karma simply because every condition has to run its course. Moment to moment we are always working with conditions. We call them problems, but they are a natural part of unfoldment.

The person who tries to bend the natural forces of life to help others could very well take on the karmic burdens of the people he has healed. There are a number of cases where a psychic healer has developed all kinds of health problems.

Most people develop health problems as they get on in years and the body begins to run down. That's a natural part of living. But those who interfere with others, without knowing the laws of Divine Spirit, take on more than is necessary.

I don't care to do it. When people come to me for healing, I don't try to heal them. I just turn it over to the Holy Spirit, the ECK. Then, if the ECK decides to heal them, great. For a little while, maybe an hour or two, the person's condition will pass through me.

Spiritual Strength

To properly walk the spiritual path, you have to be strong enough to carry your own burdens. At some point you gain the wisdom to take on fewer spiritual burdens. Soon you find that life moves along rather nicely. Not always easily, but nicely. When a problem does come up, you recognize it for what it is.

In ancient mythology there is the story of Milo of Crotona, a Greek athlete who began to build his strength by walking the streets with a baby bull calf on his shoulders. He carted it around with him every single day. As the calf increased in size and weight, Milo grew proportionately stronger, until eventually he was carrying a full-grown bull on his back.

In a way, this is also how you build strength spiritually. One day you begin to recognize that the problems in your life are of your own making. As you gain in spiritual unfoldment, you are able to create fewer problems for yourself. This is not to say that you stop having problems. Actually, as you become stronger spiritually, you graduate to a higher kind of problem.

Many probably think it must be nice to be a saint and have such happiness. But if you look at the history of the saints, you find that most of them had a life of hardship. So people long for the happiness and overlook the hardships, not putting the two components together. They don't realize that those who became saints unfolded to a higher spiritual level where, along with their greater wisdom and spiritual strength, they also had greater problems. There is a compensating balance in life.

I am not promising that if you come into ECK you're going to have fewer problems. But you will be able to handle them, and you'll also be able to handle greater problems. They'll challenge you more, but in a good way.

Recognizing the Mahanta

An ECKist in Florida had an elderly mother who used to come down to stay with her during the mild winters. The mother lived in Illinois. She was a Roman Catholic, but she also liked the writings of Billy Graham.

The daughter taught classes on ECKANKAR, and when her mother was visiting, she invited her to sit in on a few. One day the mother said, "I'm very happy you found something that gives you love and helps you grow spiritually. But the ECK teachings are too complicated for me."

The ECKist was rather puzzled by this because the teachings of ECK were perfectly clear to her. True, certain unique terms come up in the writings which may sound foreign to other people. Since the ECKist had never used those words, she was mildly offended by her mother's comment. But her mother was such a sweet, gentle person that she didn't argue the point with her.

A few years later the mother became very ill and had to be hospitalized. The ECKist went to visit her, and when it appeared that her mother was not going to recover, she arranged to stay with her until the end, which came a week later.

On several occasions it looked like the elderly woman was going to translate, or die, at any moment. She would hold her breath for about a minute and a half, until she couldn't hold it any longer. Then she would breathe out again. She did this repeatedly.

The daughter didn't know why, but each time it happened, she too would take a deep breath and hold it for as long as she could. She was that closely attuned with her mother.

The Catholic priest came and gave extreme unction. The daughter remembered that a few months earlier her mother had asked her to send a certain book by Billy Graham, as well as an ECK book. She had wondered about it at the time.

On the final day, the mother kept raising her arms up in the air, and each time they dropped to her side, she would begin to breathe again. This went on for a full day. The ECKist knew her mother was experiencing an inner struggle, but she didn't understand exactly what was going on.

At the end of this very long day, her mother suddenly

sat up in bed, looked straight ahead, and said, "Oh, Mahanta." Then she lay back down and passed away peacefully.

The daughter tried to piece all this together, and some months later she came up with this insight into what had happened. Her mother had resisted dropping the physical shell, her human body, because she hadn't made up her mind which path to follow. She was torn between the Catholic religion which she had been born into, Billy Graham to whom she'd leaned most of her life, and the teachings of ECK which she had learned about very late in life.

It wasn't important which of these paths her mother decided on as she was dying. But it was important for her to choose one. Her struggle was made harder by the fact that she had waited until the end.

Right at the final moment, she saw the Inner Master, the Mahanta. She recognized him, accepted him, and then she was able to die peacefully. It went as smoothly as it should have gone in the first place.

Never once during the week she sat at her mother's bedside did the daughter try to sway her to become an ECKist. She didn't sing HU, she didn't talk about the ECK works. She did nothing except sit there and love her mother. She realized it would have been an invasion of her mother's spiritual space if she had even imposed singing HU, the love song to God, upon her because it was not the love song that her mother was used to. Since it was her mother's decision, the daughter had to let her make up her own mind.

This is how it's supposed to be in this year of the missionary. You cannot push the teachings of ECK on people. Nor do you have to be subtle or devious about it.

If you have to do that to try to reach someone, it means two things: the person is not ready for ECK, and you probably don't know as much about ECK as you think.

"God Sent You to Me Today"

Two members of ECKANKAR own a bookstore. One of their customers is a woman in her seventies named Pearl who comes in every two weeks or so. Pearl lives on social security.

When she first began coming to the store a couple of years ago, she told the owners that she had Parkinson's disease. Even then the effects of the disease were apparent by the mild shaking. "I hope to be able to go out of this life gracefully," she said at the time. Now, two years later, she no longer thought that would be possible.

One day the store owners mentioned to Pearl that they were planning to make strawberry jam. "If you like, you can use my canner," Pearl said. "You can come home with me and pick it up." Accepting her offer, one of the owners left the store with her.

When they got to Pearl's house, she and the ECKist sat down and chatted for a while. "My home is up for sale," Pearl said. "But the way the market is right now, homes that have been listed for two years haven't sold yet." The money was needed so that she could get the proper medical care, she explained. "I have to be admitted to a home where I can have twenty-four-hour care." She was quite concerned about this.

Then she added, "The other reason I have to sell is because of my hallucinations."

Someone else might have let that comment pass, but the ECKist, being a very aware person, thought there might be more to it. "What do you mean, hallucinations?" she asked.

"Sometimes I hear my mother and father in the living room or the kitchen, just talking," Pearl said. "When I mentioned it to my doctor, he just laughed and said, 'Well, at least they're harmless hallucinations.' He didn't really believe me."

"I believe you," the ECKist said.

"Now that the time of my death is getting nearer," Pearl said, "I'm afraid of dying." The ECKist had suspected as much from comments Pearl had made in the past.

She said, "You know, there's a word you can sing, if you'd like to. It's HU, a love song to God." They talked about it for a little while, and Pearl began to ask some questions about ECKANKAR.

The ECKist then said, "The next time you hear your parents talking in another room, why not just sing HU and imagine that Jesus is in the room with them?" She was wise enough to realize that Jesus was the master to whom Pearl had looked all these years.

As the ECKist was about to leave, Pearl said to her, "God sent you to me today to teach me something that I didn't know about before. You gave me ways to lose this fear." The ECKist left then, grateful and happy that the Holy Spirit had used her as a vehicle to bring comfort and assurance to someone who really needed it.

How to Work with People as a Vahana

When you give truth to someone, you don't always have to talk about ECK this or ECK that. You work with them in terms of their state of consciousness. Pearl, a Christian for over seventy years, would have probably found it impossible to change in this life. Even if she felt close to the teachings of ECK, it would have been necessary for her to pick them up in another lifetime, if she wanted to do so.

Work with people according to their state of consciousness. If a Christian needs help and you think telling them about HU will take away some of their fear, then tell them about HU. But if you realize that it'll also give them comfort to be reminded of Jesus, then mention Jesus.

The masters work together on the inner planes. There is no conflict among them on the inner planes as there sometimes is among their followers here on earth.

A Simple Exercise

A spiritual exercise you can use whenever you go out in life is simply this: Do one good deed a day and expect no thanks for it.

It can be even the smallest deed as long as you do it for someone else, including a pet or a bird. It can be a simple kindness, like watering the plants in your home. But say to yourself, "I do this because I love you, and because God loves me." That's the only reason.

Soul exists because God loves us. There is no ulterior motive; God doesn't love us because He is going to get something out of it. So when you do a deed of love for someone else, you shouldn't expect to get anything out of it either.

This spiritual exercise will help you begin to find the happiness and satisfaction that so many are missing today in their own religions, even in ECKANKAR. They don't yet realize that to receive love, they have to give. So do a little deed of some kind for others, and you will begin to see a change in your life. You will become a happier, more fulfilled human being.

Enough Love for All

A spiritual path should be able to remake you into a person who is filled with divine love. And don't be miserly about it. If there is an opportunity to do two good deeds, don't stop at one because you have filled your quota. It's not as if you're going to use up all your love; divine love is limitless.

You find this fear even in families. A young couple get married and share love. Then the first baby comes along, and the husband feels neglected. Now that the wife is giving so much love to the baby, he thinks there won't be enough left over for him—as if there weren't enough love to go around.

There is always enough to go around. Love is the spiritual food from the granaries which are always full. If you can learn to give as much of this love as possible, you will find it returning to you in such abundance that at times you will barely be able to contain yourself.

As you go out in life, remember that you are a vehicle for the Holy Spirit, for God. You are taking the Light and Sound to people who need love. In giving it, you will receive it, and all kinds of changes will come into your life. You will find this to be true.

South Pacific Regional Seminar, Adelaide, Australia, Sunday, December 2, 1990

True prayer is the art of listening to God. In ECK, one way to open the heart is to sing HU.

7

HU—Our Love Song to God

The president has declared today a national day of prayer. The welfare of our young in the Middle East is on our minds and in our hearts. We are all concerned about their safety.

Personally, I support the actions taken in the interest of freedom. But I find it interesting when the leaders of the various nations call their citizens together for a national day of prayer to their God. It's as though there are several Gods walking around out there and each country feels it has the special ear of the real God. We know, of course, that it is the same God seen through different eyes.

Purpose of Religions

It is important to remember and understand that no human being's vision of God is a perfect vision. This is why there are so many different religions on earth. God has allowed these religions to form because each one unfolds a group of people with similar states of consciousness.

The states of consciousness within the group are not identical, of course. Each individual is on a unique path to God, and each of you has your own state of consciousness.

No matter what religion you were born into, you will try to find a group that answers your spiritual needs better than any other.

Many people do not understand that God has provided for all religions. With their imperfect vision, these people look around at the beliefs of all the other human beings on earth and conclude that, "My God is better and more powerful than your God. My God is the true God; yours is not." Because they do not recognize that God is love, they go about their daily lives trying to subdue other religions.

Did you ever wonder what God must think as He observes the folly of the human race? I sometimes imagine that He just shakes His head and says, "I shouldn't have given mankind such vanity. I never thought they'd use it against me and practice such behavior against my other children."

What Is Worship?

What is the meaning of worship? I see it as anything that brings Soul closer to God.

True worship brings Soul closer to God on Its own merits and never at the expense of someone else. You cannot bring yourself closer to God by hating others, even if you believe your anger is righteous.

The relationship between Soul—which is you—and God is one of love. Where there is pure, absolute love, there is no room for anger of any kind.

Practicing True Worship

You can tell if a person practices true worship by how he treats others throughout the week. People are very good on their holy days, but the test of true worship is how they act the other six days of the week. For me, the test of true worship is whether or not a person has charity. By that I mean goodwill toward others.

There are problems which must be dealt with here on earth, of course. Some of us agree that certain events in the Middle East should not have been allowed to go further. With memories of World War II, we feel that President Bush was right to stop a big problem before it got out of hand.

The rest of the story needs to be written. There are others who feel—probably as rightly as anyone else— that the United States does not have a right to impose its beliefs and values upon the people in other parts of the world.

Well, who's to say? I'm not here to bend anyone's thinking one way or another. My purpose is simply to say that what is important in this life is your relationship with God, and how you worship God truly. As you do this, it will show up in your daily life, whether it's your traditional holy day or not.

Charity

One of the most beautiful chapters in the Bible speaks of charity. This is from 1 Corinthians, chapter 13.

Though I speak with the tongues of men and of angels, and have not charity, I am become as sounding brass, or a tinkling cymbal.

2 And though I have the gift of prophecy, and understand all mysteries, and all knowledge; and though I have all faith, so that I could remove mountains, and have not charity, I am nothing.

3 And though I bestow all my goods to feed the poor, and though I give my body to be burned, and have not charity, it profiteth me nothing.

4 Charity suffereth long, and is kind; charity envieth not; charity vaunteth not itself, is not puffed up,

5 Doth not behave itself unseemly, seeketh not her own, is not easily provoked, thinketh no evil;

6 Rejoiceth not in iniquity, but rejoiceth in the truth;

7 Beareth all things, believeth all things, hopeth all things, endureth all things.

8 Charity never faileth: but whether there be prophecies, they shall fail; whether there be tongues, they shall cease; whether there be knowledge, it shall vanish away.

9 For we know in part, and we prophesy in part.

10 But when that which is perfect is come, then that which is in part shall be done away.

11 When I was a child I spake as a child, I understood as a child, I thought as a child: but when I became a man, I put away childish things.

12 For now we see through a glass, darkly; but then face to face: now I know in part; but then shall I know even as also I am known.

13 And now abideth faith, hope, charity, these three; but the greatest of these is charity.

The individual who knows true worship will practice this kind of charity, or goodwill, toward others.

Prayer

In the years I have been the spiritual leader of ECKANKAR, I have tried to show the members of ECK what is true prayer and what is not. True prayer lets things be. It shows trust that God has done things right. It says, "God, you're doing a good job. Everything's OK."

Wrong prayer is the kind that tries to change things, especially how other people behave. It also implies that God has fallen down on the job.

Let's say a certain person appears to drink too much. When human beings, in their vanity, feel it is necessary to pray to God about something like this, it's as if they're saying, "God, I don't know if you've noticed it, but Mr. Smith over there drinks. You remember your laws, God—he shouldn't be drinking. I'm just calling this to your attention because you probably don't have your television on."

Maybe they expect God to say, "Oh, hey, thanks a lot. I was watching the Super Bowl, and things got away from me. Glad you brought it to my attention. I'll put it through channels and see what we can do about it. Uh, don't call me, I'll call you."

This is what it amounts to when prayer is used to tell God what to do. Some actually use prayer to point out that "God, these people don't believe right." Catholics and Lutherans, for instance, do not believe in the same way, even though they look to the same God.

Seeing More Perfectly

Human beings do not yet have the perfect vision described in chapter 13 of 1 Corinthians. For now we see in part, but someday we'll see perfectly. And when the people of the world, each at their own individual states of consciousness, finally begin to see more perfectly, they will recognize each other's God as the same Being. Then they'll be able to say, "You know, there isn't such a great difference between Catholics and Lutherans after all. There

91

never was, really—not in any important way."

If there is no difference in any important way, what is all the squabble about? What are the differences, anyway? And how important are they?

When I tried to bring a new understanding of prayer to the ECKists a few years ago, it took a while. Many had been raised with the same attitude I just described. Whereas in Christianity a Catholic might pray to convert a Lutheran, or a Lutheran might pray to convert a Catholic, in ECKANKAR we had ECKists trying to convert Christians.

Because we are a new religion, most of our members have come not only from Christianity but from many of the other major religions of the world. The forming of any new religion causes a conflict. The clash between ECKists and others is reminiscent of what happened in Jesus' time between his followers and the followers of Judaism. Same thing; no difference.

Changing Consciousness

Every few centuries, or whenever the time is right, God sends Its, or His, message in a new way. The purpose is to fit the ever-unfolding consciousness of the human race.

The consciousness of mankind has changed in two thousand years, and it continues to change. As we go higher on the spiral of life, we find there is a dropping-off from some of the religions that used to serve people quite well. They worked for as long as the followers were pretty much at the same level and in tune with each other.

But when the overall consciousness has unfolded to a certain point, a new voice begins to speak, and the message God sends comes through more clearly and more attuned to the times. All of a sudden there is a division in the religious group, and even in the home, as one person can hear the still small voice and says, "I'm hearing something about spiritual things that I never heard before and always wanted to know."

Growing Up with HU

Many people in Africa now coming to ECK were raised with the sound of HU. A chant known by many of the tribes, HU, the name of God, is often used in times of trouble. When ECKANKAR came along and spoke of HU, they said, "Oh, I know about HU. I grew up with it."

Other people come to ECKANKAR because they have had experiences with the Holy Spirit, in the form of Light and Sound. In ECK we teach that the Holy Spirit is the Light and Sound of God. It is the Voice of God manifesting as Light and Sound. When people have an experience with the Light or Sound of God, in the dream state or in some other way, it changes their life.

Some have had near-death experiences in which they went briefly into the other worlds. While there, some saw the passages of Light, others heard the Sound of God. The Sound can come in many different ways, such as the music of an orchestra. Often the sound heard is so beautiful that the individual cannot speak of it.

Those who hear the inner sounds or see the inner sights usually have nothing in their religious background to explain the nature of the experience. Some stay with their religion anyway. It gives them stability and the feeling of love, and mostly a place from which to serve others.

Holy Spirit

Once you've had an experience with the Light and Sound of God, in one way or another you are going to have

93

an urge to serve. This urge is the action of charity working through you. It is the Spirit of God coming through you, trying to find Its way into this world and express Itself through you. This Spirit of God is what we call the ECK; it's no different.

People know the ECK by different names, such as the Comforter or the Holy Ghost. The Germans call it *Heilige Geist* (Holy Ghost). It makes no difference what name you give to It, whether you say it in Russian, French, or any other language. What's really important is, how do you stand with God? If you are filled with the love of God, there is only one thing you can do: Somehow, in your daily life, you must share it with others.

No matter what religion you practice, it is important that you learn to listen. This is prayer in the true sense. Again, wrong prayer is when you tell God what to do—God do this, God do that. It puts you in mind of a spouse who gets too much of that from his or her mate and just wants to say, "Please, give it a rest."

HU—Our Love Song to God

True prayer is the art of listening to God. Just open your heart and listen to God. In ECK, one way to open the heart is to sing HU. A Christian may wish to visualize Jesus.

These techniques are not meant to suggest that a Christian can't chant HU or an ECKist can't think of Jesus or anyone else. You do whatever your heart tells you to do. You are an individual, there is just one of you. You have your own understanding of God, and you are on your own path to God.

The ECK Worship Service is to help people find out what they can do to improve their relationship with God.

If we can help in any way, we are more than willing to be of service.

I would like to leave you with the blessing we usually use in ECK. It doesn't tell God to do anything. It doesn't tell you to be or to do anything differently. But it is simply accepting things as they are according to the will and the love of God, and that is: May the blessings be.

ECK Worship Service,
Temple of ECK, Chanhassen, Minnesota,
Sunday, February 3, 1991

If you can love what you are doing, you certainly have the capacity to love God. You can see it in the person who loves doing his or her work, whether it's a car salesman, a store clerk, or anyone else.

8

Feel the Love, Part 1

The war in the Persian Gulf triggered a strong recession. At first it was thought to be a regional phenomenon, but all of a sudden it was all over the place.

Just this month some of the government indexes showed that consumer spending was up by a fraction of a percent. It may be a coincidence, but that's when I bought my new suit.

Buying a Suit

The shopping process spanned several months and men's clothing stores in every city I traveled to for an ECK seminar. Figuring the sunnier climes were more likely to have the light, uplifting shade of blue I wanted, I went to stores in Florida, California, Hawaii, and Australia. Finally I found just the right thing—at home in Minnesota.

I don't know if women feel the same way, but when we men walk into a clothing store, we absolutely detest the sight of an approaching salesperson. We do not like them. The mere fact that they exist implies somehow that there is something we don't know. Most of us don't like

97

to admit to that. Besides, they tell you something fits well when it doesn't, and I don't want to spend money for something that doesn't suit me.

I worked up my nerve by watching a British comedy on TV. *Are You Being Served?* takes place in England in a clothing store called Grace Brothers. With a cast of seven or eight regular characters, all the story lines revolve around selling clothes. The head clerk, Mr. Grainger, is a dear, bumbling little man who mumbles to himself and looks like Winston Churchill past his prime.

Whenever Mr. Grainger makes a sale, he tries his best to follow the cardinal rule: do not alter anything in any way. Just convince the customer it's OK. If the customer doesn't like the fit, he sloughs it off with, "Don't worry, it'll ride up with wear."

Alterations

Eventually I found the suit I wanted and was ready to buy. But just to test the character of the salesman, I said, "I want my wife to check this out first. She'll make the final decision on whether or not I'm going to buy it."

I routinely throw in this line to car or clothing salesmen. A car salesman once made the mistake of saying, "So your wife has to make your decisions for you?" He thought he could embarrass me into buying right then and there.

"You're absolutely right," I said, and knew I wouldn't be back. I'm not going to buy from somebody who doesn't respect how a husband and wife make decisions together.

The clerk in the clothing store was a good man. He clinched the sale when he said, "Oh, that's perfectly all right. I understand just how it is."

So I took the suit home to show my wife.

Because it was seminar time and my wife and I were both busy, I went back for alterations alone.

I tried on the suit so he could measure it for the alterations. "I'm not sure that the coat sleeves are long enough," I said.

"Just depends on what you like," he said, arranging his features into a doubtful expression. "I had a customer try on a coat the other day. The sleeves hung down to the middle of his thumbs, and he thought they were just perfect."

It was obvious he didn't want to make any adjustments to the coat. "I'd like it to fit just right," I insisted.

"Well, we can let out the seams in the back a little bit," he agreed. Then he launched into another story about a customer who tried on a coat that fit him like a bag. "But it was just what the man wanted," he said, "and I suppose it looked just fine to him."

I began to get the picture: Don't worry, it'll ride up with wear.

The trousers, of course, had to be cuffed and shortened. He asked if I wanted a little break in them. When I said yes, he did something to them that made them look just terrible. But he was the expert, so I didn't say anything. Men are supposed to know everything, but once the experts speak, we turn to mush and buy the worst junk you ever saw. Then our wives say, "Why didn't you say something?" You just can't explain these things to them.

But I enjoyed the salesman. Not only did I see the Light of God coming through him, I also understood his point of view. Wanting the suit to fit properly was my own idiosyncrasy. He doesn't get paid extra for tailoring once a suit is sold, so why encourage it?

He cinched my future business a few days later by

sending me a thank-you card. It said, "I very much appreciated your business, and I hope to see you back again." That, I thought, is a very smart salesman. And I will go back again, simply because he cared enough to send me a card.

Feel the Love

The title of this talk, "Feel the Love," refers to the love that comes from other people. As you go about in your everyday life, you may not find a lot of people who are filled with love or who take the time to show it.

With the restrictions of business and the pressure to keep on schedule, many feel there is no time to be human. No time to let others know, "Hey, I like you. We have to do business now, but we might as well enjoy each other's company for a few minutes too." Those who do have this attitude are open to life. It's as if they are reflecting the love of God, and indeed, this truly is what they are doing.

You can see it in the person who loves doing his or her work, whether it's a car salesman, a store clerk, or anyone else. If you can love what you are doing, you certainly have the capacity to love God. And if you can love God, you can love another person. The teachings of ECK are to open your heart to love, and this is not always easy.

Finding a Tailor

When the alterations were completed, I brought the suit home and put it on to show my wife. "Oh, no," I said, looking at the fit of the trousers. "It looks like I'm standing in two gunnysacks. I can't wear these."

The store where I bought the suit offered free tailoring, but I couldn't bring myself to go back there and ask for it.

Finally I took the suit to another tailor, a gentleman from the Middle East. He was a little defensive at first, but I understood why. Although the war in the Persian Gulf was over, during its short duration many people of Middle Eastern background felt persecution in this country. All the trust they had earned up to that point didn't seem to matter. As soon as the war began, some Americans built walls between the differences—he talks with an accent, his skin is a different color, and so on.

I explained what was wrong with the pants and he took my measurements. "Just a little break?" he said.

"Yes, just a little break."

My wife had pointed out something to me. The salesman who sold me the suit was an older gentleman from another age when men wore their trousers baggy. She said, "When he asked you if you wanted a little break in the trousers, he was talking a different language than you were." So when I told this tailor, "Just a little break," I watched to see what he would do, and he did it right. We were on the same wavelength.

Seeing the Light of Love

I don't think he spoke English very well because he didn't say much, but he sure knew how to tailor clothing. His detached, businesslike manner gave the impression of a very hard human being inside the skin.

"Wonderful rain we've been having," I said.

"Yes, but we're supposed to have sunshine tomorrow," he replied. That seemed to perk him up a bit. A person from the Middle East would be more used to sunshine, whereas I viewed the rain as relief from the drought.

101

As soon as we began to talk about a neutral subject, he brightened. And in his eyes I saw the light of love. They reflected the gentle humor of a very loving human being.

As I go about my everyday life, doing errands or whatever, more than anything else I appreciate the opportunity to find the person through whom this Light of God is shining.

Off Track

I spend a lot of time looking at what I call the spiritual psychology of people. Occasionally I observe someone, even in ECK, getting off track. But when this happens, the person who is off track generally doesn't know it. This is one of the great mysteries of life.

ECKists have said to me, "If I ever get out of balance, please tell me." But I've learned that it would only hurt them if I said so. When people are out of balance, they simply don't know what to do to get back in balance.

Years ago, when I first got this position, I sometimes had the audacity to say to someone, "You're out of balance." Good meddler that I was, I would then try to point out how he was out of balance.

The person usually became defensive and proceeded to explain to me why he was not out of balance at all. Finally I decided not to meddle anymore.

I have found that the best course of action is to let people run their course. If a situation gets too far out of hand, I'll do what I can to lift it to a higher level than it was before.

Purifying Process

Those who have shut themselves off from ECK have also shut themselves off from love. They often become

102

suspicious, sometimes to the point of paranoia. The most insignificant comment convinces them that other people are out to harm them, to take something away from them. It's a very interesting phenomenon.

When a person is in this mind-set, there is nothing on earth either you or I can do to overcome it. But the ECK then begins to give them certain experiences, not to punish but to purify.

Lest this sound as if these are rare, isolated cases, I want to point out that it happens to everybody in ECK. Each of you in turn passes through a time of purification as the Holy Spirit, the ECK, brings you lessons from your past in a new form. It feeds them back to you for breakfast, lunch, and dinner until finally you get so stuffed that you simply can not take any more.

This is when you say, "I've got to go on a diet from all that." All of a sudden you begin to reexamine where you have been and what you have done, not just to yourself but to others.

Total Responsibility

It's one thing if we go out of balance and destroy ourself—through alcohol, gluttony, or whatever. Sometimes we feel helpless to turn it around, and so we let the problem run our life.

But more often than not we also affect the well-being of those around us. A spouse might say, "I love my mate, but he or she becomes a totally different person under the influence of alcohol."

Nowadays drinking is called a disease. Many of our actions are given gimmicky names that deny or ignore what they really are. It's the way of psychology to throw the responsibility onto some cause other than the person

103

himself. One of the reasons is because medical insurance does not cover anything that is not called a disease. Therefore, if someone decides that a certain treatment is necessary for a person to overcome a habit, clever labeling can be used to submit the costs to the insurance company.

I'm probably going to get a lot of flack for these statements. There will be letters of protest that say, "This is a real disease, and there are other conditions that are also real diseases." But I have seen too many people who were once alcoholics stop drinking. They did it because people have the ability to decide to stop.

On the other hand, a condition like cancer is a disease in that no amount of ordinary willpower can produce the same effect. It's not a situation where you can just say, "I have cancer today but I've decided not to have it tomorrow."

I'm making a distinction between a valid physical disease and an inclination which society has labeled a disease for convenience. I'm talking about total responsibility.

Community Spirits

Growing up, I found myself in a position similar to what many others go through. I grew up in a community of farmers of German background. As we worked each day on our family farm, we got a lot of dust in our throats. I suppose the fizzy water produced by an Alka-Seltzer could have cleared our throats, but German farmers don't drink Alka-Seltzer—they drink beer.

I never considered myself an alcoholic. None of us did. It's just that beer was good for washing down the dust—starting at noon each day. If we were in the dead of winter and there was no dust to be seen, we still washed it down with that bottle of beer. Unless, of course, there were other farmers visiting. Then we might have two bottles.

Another one was needed by midafternoon, of course, because when you're working hard, you've got to get that dust down. The bottle of beer with supper was needed to clear away the day's accumulation, and later, just in case there was any dust left from yesterday, we drank more to get it all down.

The only time a person in our community was suspected of being an alcoholic was if he had his first beer before noon. We may have thought he was on the verge of a problem, but nobody was willing to say for sure. Maybe he just had more dust.

Peer Pressure

In some communities alcohol plays a very strong role in how you relate to other members of your family, your neighbors, and so on. It's something you have in common with everyone else. If you don't drink with them, then all of a sudden they don't love and accept you as they did before; and if they cut off the love, you can't exist in the group.

So now you have a choice: Give up this common interest and lose the love and respect of the others, or keep doing it and continue to be accepted. Or maybe you cut back but fake it when others are around: you drink tea and make believe it's the hard stuff.

I had a very difficult time when I decided to give up beer. Paul Twitchell had said that, by the Second Initiation, an ECKist should be free of alcohol. If this was going to help me spiritually, then I was going to do it, come hell or high water.

One day my dad and I went to an elderly neighbor's farm to help with some of the chores. When we went in the house for a break, the farmer opened the refrigerator, and without even asking, he uncorked a beer and handed it to me.

"I'd rather not have a beer," I said.

"You what?" He looked at me as if I had slapped him. I guess I had, in a way, but I didn't know what else to do. My dad was embarrassed to have this neighbor know his son would not drink beer, so it was very awkward for all of us.

Many of you face the same pressures and more, especially if you are in the service. I remember how it was when I joined the air force. Along with the green fatigues, it was as if we were issued these instructions: You may drink as soon as you get out of boot camp. Peer pressure practically makes it a requirement.

In spite of all these obstacles, what I'm saying is: feel the love. Feel it as it flows through other people. If they seem less than perfect, it's because they are very human. They are not God-Realized, they are not Self-Realized. In fact, half the time most people find it hard enough just putting one foot in front of the other and trying to take care of themselves.

When Game Plans Change

We all have a hard time in this life. Why? Because somebody keeps changing the game plan. You were employed at the same company for years, your future was all mapped out, then all of a sudden you lost your job. Government contracts were cut back, and you were one of the casualties. Who changed the game plan? Who called for this recession? What do you do now?

Most people live from paycheck to paycheck. Now that you don't have one coming in, you can't make the mortgage payments. You go to the bank and try to refinance the loan, but since the bankers are having their own troubles, you may not get the help you want. You don't always find that helpful, friendly spirit through whom you wish the Light of God would shine.

You find instead that if the Light is going to come through anybody in these hard times, it has to be you. Everybody else has his shutters closed. They too are just trying to survive and figure out, How do I keep all the material possessions that I bought on credit? We all want the good things for our family and for ourself.

Another Level of Love

We held the first worship service in the Temple of ECK a couple of weeks ago. Some of the visitors who came weren't in ECK, and they said, "We thought you would be a little more radical than you are."

At the worship service I read from 1 Corinthians 13. It's a very short chapter on love.

I read this as a bridge of understanding for the people who came to the ECK Worship Service, so that they would find something that was familiar and holy to them. There are many passages in the Christian Bible that we also recognize as poetic, beautiful truths.

In ECK we are trying to take mankind's yearning for love one step further, to another level. The traditional religions were formed, and then they developed their doctrines and dogmas. Over a period of time these doctrines and dogmas became set in stone. But the overall consciousness has expanded since then. In the fast-changing times of today, the churches are out of step, hard-pressed to answer the spiritual needs of the people. They have very little, if any, information about the Sound and Light of God.

Strengthening the Love Within

The whole reason we are here is to find the Sound and Light of God. And what is the Sound and Light? It's the Holy Spirit, the ECK. And what is ECK? ECK is love, God is love. This is what we are looking for. We're looking for this bridge between divine love and the state we are in today. How do we find it? By ridding ourselves of the things that impede or hinder us on the way to this divine love.

Some people stagger along under the weight of unnecessary baggage like gluttony, alcoholism, and so on. To unload these burdens and make our path to God straighter, we start with the things that we can do something about. If we take this initiative, the Holy Spirit comes in and helps with the rest.

The effort we make shows that we are indeed Godbeings. For each of us is Soul, a spark of God. As such, we have the divinity within ourselves to say, "I long to be united with the Sound and Light, to be together with that which is love."

People often lie to each other, mostly because they no longer trust each other. The reason they have stopped trusting is because they've let this element of divine love within them break down. They've let other things get in the way.

When a person can no longer love, he sinks into a state of suspicion and mistrust. Problems begin to crop up in his life, multiplying to the point where he feels backed against the ropes, like in a boxing ring. This is when he cries out, "God, help me!"

Often it's the way of the divine power to say, "OK, but let's see you try to pick yourself up first." That's how it works. God won't do for you what you won't do for yourself.

It's understood that you are human, you don't have all the answers, and so you can't do everything for yourself. But you have to be willing to try. And if you try, with trust in the principle of love, which is Divine Spirit, then the forces of life converge to help you reach the purification you need to find meaning and understanding in the events in this life.

The Flow of ECK

An ECK seminar is an opportunity to get to know each other and to renew old friendships. It is not enough to come just to fill yourself up on mental stimulation from the talks, including mine, and think this is the purpose of being here. That's not it at all.

The heart of the seminar experience is feeling the divine love that comes through on an occasion such as this. The ECK flow is stronger than usual when we all get together. You can then carry some of this love home with you after the weekend is over.

May the blessings be.

ECK Springtime Seminar, Washington, D.C., Friday, March 29, 1991

He showed her how to measure and cut the paper properly and make it adhere to the walls. She had asked the ECK for help by singing HU. Suddenly the help began to come—and it was very specialized help.

9

Feel the Love, Part 2

The ECK book *Earth to God, Come In Please...* is a collection of experiences shared by ECKists who have felt the presence of the Holy Spirit, the ECK, in their lives. Their stories illustrate how the ECK not only brings help and guidance in times of need, but works in all aspects of one's life.

There is a mystery about the nature of the ECK and how It works. Also known as the Holy Ghost or the Comforter, in Christianity It is spoken of as a person. But that is not what It is. In ECK we know It as the Sound Current.

Hearing HU

The two aspects of the ECK are Light and Sound. The word HU is one of the aspects of the Sound, but you may also hear It in a number of other ways in the course of your daily life.

One of the ways is right here in the hotel. A sound very similar to that of a HU Chant seems to circulate through the ventilation system of this building. It's as if the sound of HU is rolling through the hotel all the time, showing you how to sing a love song to God in a very nice way. It isn't often that we come across a hotel that can sing HU, but this is one of them.

Upset Driver

Something keeps happening to me that demonstrates how important it is to feel the love. The reoccurring incidents take place at stores, the post office, or wherever there's a parking lot, and a woman is involved every time. I'm not sure, but it could be the same woman in different disguises.

I have no idea why she follows me around, but I know she's out there. I can always tell it's her because whenever she does something wrong, she blames me. And when she does something out of ignorance, she blames me for that too. It's getting to the point where I'm scared to go any place where I might run into her.

She's about fifty-five years old, taller than I am, and quite hefty. Not only does she carry a lot of opinions with her, but she makes sure that I hear them. She's the kind of person you want to go up to and say, "Feel the love" — but she'd probably deck you.

The first time I met her was on my way into the parking lot of a store. I had just made a right turn onto the long driveway that leads to the parking lot. At the same time, the traffic on the opposite side of the street, facing me, began their left turn into the parking lot.

The first car pulled past me on the left, then the second car. Although there was no center line, the driveway was wide, and there was plenty of room.

I was driving along, minding my own business, when all of a sudden I heard a horn blasting behind me. I don't like it when people honk their horns at me; it makes me want to slam on my brakes. Fighting off the impulse, I looked in the left rearview mirror to see what's going on, and there she was—in a white Cadillac, cruising on my back bumper.

She could easily have pulled around me in the huge driveway, but she was too upset. I found out later that she felt I had cut in front of her when I turned right at the light. It didn't matter that I had pulled into the driveway before she even made her turn, or that there were two other cars ahead of her in her lane—it was my fault. She wanted to speed into the parking lot, and I was in the way. Blasting her horn one more time for effect, she accelerated and roared past me.

Now I was upset too. I watched as she parked her car, got out, slammed the door shut, and broke into a run. She was in a real hurry to get to the store. As I drove past her, I reached over and lowered the passenger window. "You probably didn't notice," I said very calmly, "but the freeway is over there."

That was not the thing to say. She gave me a ferocious glare, then proceeded to bat my ears down. The waves of anger poured out of her so strongly that I was actually shaking. When she finally left I thought, "This is unbelievable."

If you have ever been around a very angry person, you know what it feels like. Without even realizing it, you begin to shake. It's a reaction to the kind of energy that is being thrown out. We also emit good energy, such as love. But when a person becomes very angry, the force is so strong that you can almost reach out in the air and pinch it. And sometimes you have to pinch it before it pinches you.

After that first encounter, I called home to talk to my

wife, just to get balanced out. A two-minute call was all it took. Then I continued with my errands. It's best to get away from someone who is so out of control of their emotions.

At the Post Office

Similar incidents happened a couple of times at the post office. Many of the post offices in the Minneapolis area were built several decades ago. The population has doubled or tripled since then, but the parking lots have stayed the same size.

This particular branch office is located on a well-traveled four-lane street. It's often so busy that the cars are lined up in the street, holding up traffic as they wait their turn to pull in.

One day I was third in line. Since my car was half in the street, I kept glancing nervously over my right shoulder to make sure there wasn't a fast vehicle coming behind me. For some reason the woman in the first car in line did not notice that two parking spots were available. I could see them from my car. Sometimes you have to do some creative parking in that lot, but apparently she didn't know that.

The driver of the second car finally got tired of sitting. He pulled around car number one and eased into the first parking spot. I waited for a minute, but the woman in the first car still didn't move. I figured she must be waiting for someone inside the post office, so I pulled around in front of her too.

On the other side of the lot were several delivery trucks lined up in a row. The post office doesn't object when patrons double-park behind them. Once the trucks have returned from making their deliveries, they don't have to leave again until the next day.

A car that had been double-parked behind a truck pulled away. I drove up to take his place but there wasn't enough room to pull in. Just then a car behind me moved out, so I backed up to get his spot.

Then I heard a horn honking to my left. I looked over and saw that car number one had decided to get into the game and find a parking space. It was obvious she didn't know the conventions of the parking lot because she had pulled right past another available space to get to me.

The driver's glare made it clear that she was not too pleased with me. "Oh, boy," I thought. "What didn't I do right today?"

I got out of the car and had to walk right past her. She wasn't about to let me off the hook. Rolling down her window, she leaned out and screeched at the top of her lungs, "You deliberately edged me out of that parking space!" I was just amazed that a human being could be so loud.

"No, that wasn't the case at all," I said, and tried to explain that I thought she had been waiting for someone to come out of the post office. She didn't buy it.

I went inside, got my mail, and by the time I came out she had found a space and had just gotten out of her car. We met again right in the middle of the parking lot. She came huffing up, taller than me and itching for a fight. It seemed prudent to apologize for the misunderstanding. That calmed her down long enough for me to get away.

It wasn't completely her fault that she didn't know the rules of the parking lot. These places have become like a chicken coop with too many chickens. When people feel crowded and rushed, they don't bother to let the love come through.

Love or Anger?

But once again the same woman—or maybe it was her sister—had unleashed her anger at me over her own mistake. Even when I tried to appease her, she had too much pride to back down from what she had already said, so she tried to keep up her show of anger.

About two weeks later, when the incident should have been long gone from my memory, I went back to the post office. I pulled in the parking lot and drove to the far side to double-park behind the mail trucks. There were no empty spaces, but this time I didn't hang around. I knew that woman was waiting for me. It didn't matter that I couldn't see her—I knew she was there.

Whenever another person loses their temper, we have a chance to respond either with anger or with love and charity. It's not always easy to show charity to someone who has just flattened your ears. Sometimes it takes a real effort to feel the love.

The Man Who Met Paul Twitchell

I recently spoke with a gentleman who knew Paul Twitchell, the modern-day founder of ECKANKAR, many years ago. They met in a coffee shop in Ocean Beach, California, where they were both regular customers.

Every morning Paul would talk to him about the teachings of ECKANKAR. The man didn't understand any of it because he had never before come across the spiritual concepts Paul was trying to tell him about.

"It's funny," the man told me, "but whenever we can't understand where another person is coming from, it's the easiest thing in the world just to call him a nut."

He's right. If you disagree with someone's politics or beliefs, it's very easy to call him a political nut, a health nut, a religious nut, and so on. But applying a derogatory label to another person says more about you than it does about him. It shows that you are unable to express the love which is your divine birthright, or bestow it upon this individual who has the same heritage that you do. You are Soul, you know that; but when someone makes you angry or expresses different views, does it cross your mind that he or she is also Soul?

So morning after morning this man listened to Paul talk about ECKANKAR, and it didn't make any sense to him. One day Paul said to him, "You're just not ready for ECKANKAR. Go out in the world and look for whatever it is you're looking for, and maybe someday you'll find it."

That was the last time they saw each other. But a few minutes after Paul left, a feeling of ecstasy came over the man. "I had never felt like that before in my life," he said. "The answers to all the questions I'd ever had were sparkling clear. I was in a state of euphoria."

The euphoria he felt was the love of God, and he spent many years looking for a way to recapture it. Finally, almost twenty years after meeting Paul Twitchell, the man became a member of ECK.

Some people are critical of Paul. He was up to shenanigans for most of his life. But once he realized his mission, ECKANKAR became his breath, his life force. He lived it and spoke of it constantly, day and night. Those who were receptive to it and understood what he was saying got the gift of love. Often even those who didn't understand got the gift of love.

Hanging Wallpaper

One way to open yourself up to help from the ECK, or the Holy Spirit, is to sing the word *HU*. An ECKist in

Florida saw how this worked. She decided to wallpaper the bedroom while her husband was out of town.

Full of confidence, she laid out all her materials and got started. All she had to do was measure and cut the wallpaper, brush on the paste, and hang the paper. She'd have those walls covered in no time.

But as soon as she got to work, everything began to go wrong. First she couldn't get the measurements right. Then, when she applied the adhesive and flattened the first strip of paper against the wall, it immediately came loose and fell to the floor.

She tried another piece, and the same thing happened. She just could not get the paper to stick. Soon she was surrounded by fallen wallpaper.

Finally it occurred to her that it might help if she sang HU. It was worth a try. She chanted HU for a while, then tried to put the wallpaper up again. It went a little better, but some of the cut pieces still did not fit. Frustrated, she realized that it would take all day to finish the job.

She was standing ankle-deep in scrap pieces and damp strips of wallpaper when the phone rang. It was an old friend that she hadn't heard from in a year.

"Guess what," the friend said. "I'm working with a contractor now. I'm hanging wallpaper." You have to admit, this isn't something that happens every day.

The ECKist explained her predicament, and the friend was able to give her a number of tips. After she hung up, she went back to work. Again, it went a little better but not much. So the woman kept singing HU to herself.

All of a sudden the doorbell rang. "Oh, great," she muttered. "Just what I need." She opened the door to find a Jehovah's Witness standing there, ready to launch into his pitch.

118

She said, "I have to apologize but I just can't talk with you. I'm hanging wallpaper."

"Wallpaper!" he said. "That used to be my profession."

When the ECK sends help, you don't turn it away. She immediately invited him to come in.

He showed her how to measure and cut the paper properly and make it adhere to the walls. They chatted while they worked, and soon the bedroom was decorated with smooth, even strips of new wallpaper.

Constant Presence of ECK

Later she thought about how it had all worked out. She had asked the ECK for help by singing HU. Suddenly the help began to come—and it was very specialized help.

When you sing HU, the Holy Spirit begins to work in your life. It begins to change the situation with which you are struggling.

You may not readily see the results you expected, but in one way or another you will find that It is working with you. A sudden insight may show you that the problem is not with the wallpaper, but with you. In other words, maybe you had to go through the difficulty to learn something about yourself.

People often overlook the constant presence of the Holy Spirit, the ECK, in their lives. In ECKANKAR you try to become more aware of how you and the Holy Spirit are working with each other every day. The ECK is always here; It is always with you.

Mahanta Consciousness

The Mahanta Consciousness that we speak of in ECK is similar to the principle of the Christ consciousness in

Christianity. Christ is a state of consciousness. It's an inner force at a certain level.

When St. Paul said, "If any man be in Christ, he is a new creature," he was referring to this state of consciousness. More than just having your mind fixed on something, it means that you live and breathe that state of consciousness.

It's not something you can define, it's something you must live. And the way to live it is to surrender to the divine force, to the Holy Spirit. You not only say, "Thy will be done," you live and breathe those words.

In ECK we do this by learning to live and breathe the word *HU*. It's an old name for God that will help you through the most troubled times in your life. When it seems there is no help or love from anyone around you, remember to sing HU. This can fill you with love and give you the insight to see what you need to know about yourself.

As you learn more about HU, you will learn more about yourself as a spiritual being, as Soul.

ECK Springtime Seminar, Washington, D.C.,
Saturday, March 30, 1991

Every now and then, put yourself on the edge of life. Take a chance. If you're afraid to talk in front of an audience, try it anyway.

10

Awaken to ECK

As ECKANKAR grows, we might occasionally borrow various practices and songs from here and there. They will be contemporary in nature. If a song is spiritual in content and we found it uplifting before, we might enjoy singing it in ECK too. "Amazing Grace" is a beautiful public-domain song that is being adapted to express the ECK viewpoint.

Most people sing the words to songs without much thought. A phrase that comes to mind is "to save a wretch like me." They think, "Ah, a wretch like me," nobly identifying themselves as a real wretch in need of God's mercy to save them. They don't realize that actually this is a form of vanity.

Curious Mix

Today is the celebration of Easter for Christians. As a child raised in a Christian family, I wasn't too concerned about being saved. On Easter morning I might have felt relieved at the idea that Christ rose from the dead. But what really made me ecstatic was when the Easter bunny got off his nest.

The church established the doctrine of "Christ is risen." It also incorporated some of the old pagan beliefs, such as the Easter bunny and its eggs. These were symbols of fertility borrowed from an ancient seasonal ritual.

Church doctrine has always lived side by side with pagan beliefs. But most of us grew up not questioning this curious mix. We accepted the fact that Christ and the Easter bunny shared the same day. As children we probably felt a little more reverence for the Easter bunny.

Turning Things Around

Everything has seemed backward to me this weekend. As I mentioned last evening, this hotel, with the sound of HU rolling through the ventilation system, is wonderful. But our room was another story. It felt like it was laid out in reverse. No matter which way I turned, whatever I was looking for was on the opposite side of the room.

The beds were confusing too. For the first two nights we slept in the one on the left. All night long I kept waking up every few minutes. Either my left elbow, fingers, toes, or feet would be asleep. I would turn over, stretch, and try to get back to sleep. By the time the alarm went off, I was exhausted just from stretching.

Finally I told my wife, "No matter what, we're going to sleep in the other bed tonight. It can't be any worse than this one, and even if it is, I don't care."

To prove my point I did a comparison test. First I patted the mattress on the old bed then on the new. They both felt firm enough so I went to the next level—the bounce test. Standing next to the old bed, I flopped down with all my weight and bounced five times. Then I turned around and did the same on the other bed—eight bounces.

"They feel the same to me," my wife said. But she had only applied the pat test.

"No," I said, "there's a difference of three bounces between them. That much of a difference is worth a try." I've been sleeping pretty well since we switched.

What's Going On Here?

Even last night's talk came out backward. My intention was to start with the subject of love and end with a spiritual exercise involving the sound of HU in the hotel. But then I heard myself start out with comments about the hotel. I thought, I can't believe I'm saying this. From that point on, the talk seemed to unwind in reverse order. I probably should have walked off the stage backward, just to keep pace with the rest of the experience.

The ECK works through me to show the ECK-Vidya constantly. Sometimes there is no rest, no peace. When something is revealed for my own realization during a talk, it can be very unsettling. My mind then starts to work on the bigger issue: What's going on here? So last night I had two or three trains of thought going on while I gave the talk. I was working hard.

Finally I realized what the strange events of this weekend were all about. The ECK was showing me, through the ECK-Vidya, what we had to do in ECKANKAR in the future.

Learning a New Way

We did things a certain way during our first twenty-five years of development. But the Temple of ECK represents a dividing line between the past and the future. We are going to have to learn a new way to present the

125

teachings of the Sound and Light to the world.

In the old days there was a joy in the missionary effort as we went out and told people about ECK. We have to find that spirit again. Somewhere along the way we became almost an introverted group who talked mostly to ourselves. We grew so accustomed to using our own peculiar semantics—such as *Arahata* instead of *teacher*—that nobody else knew what we were talking about.

These are sacred words that have a special meaning to us when we talk among ourselves. But we also used them to explain ECK to people who didn't have the foggiest notion what they meant. To them it sounded like mumbo jumbo. This is the mode we had gotten into more and more right up to the building of the Temple of ECK.

Spirit of Love

The Temple signifies a whole new era for ECKANKAR. We talk about many different things in ECK. But always in the background, standing right behind it all, is this love current, the Life Stream of ECK. The teachings of God boil down to the enjoyment of life and the spirit of loving life. It always gets back to love, life, and loving life.

Each of you now has to reexamine yourself and try to recapture that spirit of love and adventure. This is the challenge for everyone in ECK, from the staff at the ECKANKAR Spiritual Center to the RESAs, the Higher Initiates, and all the ECK initiates. It's going to be a time of rediscovery.

A very dear ECKist wrote to me, "Harold, please don't say any more about those who are not ready to go further in ECK or who have problems with ECKANKAR as a religion. I like ECKANKAR as a religion. Let's just go forward and enjoy this life."

I agree. Enough is enough. But for every hundred letters written in this vein, I receive one from someone who is having a problem with the changes. I would prefer that we not dwell in the past. But when I am directed to address this, I have to do it.

Awaken to ECK

We have to try to awaken to this new spirit in ECK. One way to do this is to recapture the moment. If the ECK gives you an urge or a prompting to do something, don't put it off; go and do it now.

It could be as simple as a nudge to write an entry in your spiritual journal. Don't say, "Oh, I'll remember that. I'll do it later." Because as surely as you put it off, the idea will pass away.

Or you might have a prompting where you say, "It's been a while since I've led a book discussion or given an introductory talk on ECKANKAR. I used to find it fun, but it's scary."

Do something once in a while that frightens you a little bit. Sometimes life gets too comfortable. If it goes on like that for too long, it becomes numbing. There is no real enjoyment. This is when you might tend to say, "Life is such a drag. ECKANKAR has gotten dull." It isn't ECKANKAR that's gotten dull; you have gotten dull.

Some of you have received a letter from the ECKANKAR Spiritual Center inviting you to give a talk at a major seminar. How did you react? Did you clutch your chest in fear and scream, "No! I'm not ready for that!" Maybe you're not. But why not consider speaking at a smaller event, such as a regional seminar?

Every now and then, put yourself on the edge of life. Take a chance. If you're afraid to talk in front of an audience, try it anyway. Just once, participate in an ECK program and speak to a large group of people. The thought of it might scare you to death, but I guarantee you, you'll feel more alive after that talk than you did before.

Challenge yourself to do things you have gotten too comfortable to try. Don't say, "I'm a Higher Initiate now, and people will see me make a fool of myself." So what? I do it all the time.

ECK-Vidya

The ECK-Vidya works through you in the same way that it works through me. Known in ECKANKAR as the ancient science of prophecy, it is not limited to glimpses into the future. The past, present, and future are tied together.

We might be given a look into a past life to gain greater insight into why certain things are happening to us today. This may show us that unless we change the patterns from the past, the problems in our life today are going to continue tomorrow. The ECK-Vidya gives us a fuller picture of how the patterns of the past affect the present and future.

There was a time when I was very interested in knowing the future. I had some success because I put a lot of attention on it. I do the same thing now, but there's a difference.

Like any other human being, I have my own opinions about how certain things should or will go in the future. You can flip a coin and do as well as I do when working that way. But sometimes the ECK comes through and shows me something I had absolutely no idea about. It could be a future occurrence or something that is going on right now.

Just Be Open

Things like this make you realize that you are not always very smart. On the other hand, to serve ECK well, you don't have to be smart. You just have to be open.

Our society often puts too much weight on intelligence. There is nothing wrong with knowledge; I study all the time. But most people who study life consider themselves students because they feel they know so little. They find that the more they learn, the less they know.

If you feel a prompting from the ECK, even about something so commonplace as jotting a note in your spiritual journal, just do it; don't think about it. If you don't have half an hour to spend on it, then just take ten minutes and write down a short version of whatever thoughts come through.

The Lost Discourse

I usually write one discourse a month, starting on a weekend and continuing through the week until it's finished. Recently I began the preliminary work on a new discourse series for third-year students. I could see very clearly what the ECK was telling me to put down. So I jotted some notes in preparation for the actual writing.

Something else came up that required more immediate attention. Not wanting to do both at once, I put aside the discourse and got to work on the other project. No problem, I thought. I have my notes. As soon as the other thing is completed, I'll get right back to it.

I finished the other project, then gathered my notes for what was supposed to be the second discourse in the series. I now call it the lost discourse. Spreading out the notes next to the typewriter, I looked them over. They made absolutely no sense at all.

My wife offered to go over them with me. "It's no use," I said. "They just don't make any sense."

The ECK had manifested something for me to put down in written form at that particular time and place. But the window remained open only for a period of perhaps two days while I worked on my research notes. And then it shut. After that point the notes meant nothing.

Trust the ECK

A similar incident happened during the talk last night. I brought along the notes I had made for the previous night's talk but hadn't used. When I got here and scanned my notes, they no longer meant anything to me. So besides giving the talk backward, I had to make up about three-quarters of it as I sat onstage.

I had to make a great effort. And if you love ECK, you are going to make the effort too. You'll do things even when you're scared half out of your mind. You might even find yourself in a tight spot, not knowing what to do next. You can only say, "OK, what now?"

Trust the ECK to take you one step more. Just take the first step, then the next step. If you're in the middle of a talk and nothing comes, then have the group go into contemplation or something. There is always a way.

How to Serve

Four points came through the ECK-Vidya on how we can best serve the ECK. This is how one can awaken to the new spirit of ECK—to the spirit within that may have died and needs to be resurrected.

To best serve the ECK:

First, always clear a path to the ECK teachings for others.

Second, keep your distance; be detached; and be fair in your dealings with others.

If you are in a leadership position, you have to be absolutely fair with those who look to you for leadership. For instance, in situations where you have to make a decision between two people—one you love dearly and one you don't know—weigh the issue very carefully. Don't let your personal feelings get in the way.

By distancing yourself from your feelings, you will be able to move in the direction of the spiritual viewpoint and see the situation more from the Soul consciousness—the seat of Soul.

To make this work out in your daily life, whether you are a leader in ECK or not, just be fair in your dealings with others. Whenever there is an issue at hand, be fair. This will do more than gain you respect; it will open you to the mutual respect of Soul for Soul.

Only with Love

Third, serve ECK only out of love.

Don't do it to make points or have someone pat you on the back; it doesn't work that way. Very seldom does the ECK pat me on the back and say, "Job well done, Harold!"

There are moments when I need reassurance, and I don't always get it. But then the ECK shows me, in some way, that what I am doing is part of a bigger plan. The reinforcement is needed because sometimes I get so involved in the day-to-day dealings that I too forget to see the overview. This is how it is.

If I'm shattering any myths about how the ECK works or what the Living ECK Master knows or does not know, that's too bad. Remember, I'm trying to do my best too.

Absolute Patience

Fourth, have absolute patience.

You can find a way to always clear a path to the ECK teachings for others, be fair, and serve ECK only out of love; but more than any of these, you need to practice absolute patience. I speak from experience.

Living Ideals

There is a lot of history here in Washington, D.C. There's the Lincoln Memorial, the Jefferson Memorial, and the Washington Monument. The monuments and memories of someone from the past mean nothing. What counts are the living ideals that they represent even today.

What did these memorialized people stand for? How did they follow the Spirit of ECK? Lincoln and Washington certainly had a difficult time keeping awake to the ECK, but in their own way, they did it. Any leader in history who accomplished something of positive value was awake to ECK.

You too can be great in spirit and great in ECK. Keep your heart open to love. As you go home, I am always with you. And I love you.

ECK Springtime Seminar, Washington, D.C.,
Sunday, March 31, 1991

In ECK, both men and women conduct services. The word of God is in the heart of each of us.

11

The Light and Sound of God

The May 1991 issue of *Reader's Digest* carried an item about an ecumenical group of doctoral students comparing notes on sermon preparation. One minister said that he devoted the month of July to writing all his sermons for the year.

That's fifty-two sermons, plus weddings, funerals, and special holidays. What a tremendous workload that must be, I thought.

Another minister said that he outlined the sermon on Mondays and completed it during the week. A rabbi explained that he set aside Wednesday mornings to make sure it would be ready in time, while a Catholic priest admitted that he rushed to meet his deadline by working late on Saturday night. That seemed kind of risky to me.

When the discussion came around to the Episcopal minister, he fidgeted for a minute, then finally said, "Well, I usually schedule a long hymn before the sermon."

That really is trusting in God to come across with a message at the last minute.

Life's Pressures

It's important to remember that the Light and Sound of God are with us in our daily lives. There is a great deal of stress in life, especially in the U.S. now that the country is in a recession. Some say we're halfway out of it. Others say we have only taken the first step. Either way, there's a long dark road through the forest before the effects of coming out of it will be felt.

For now, it's harder to balance the checkbook. We still need food. We want to maintain the standard of living to which we grew accustomed during the glorious eighties, a decade of strong materialism. The economy seemed so strong under President Reagan. But now they tell us the national debt and personal debt in our country have risen to new levels.

This puts pressure on people. It shows up in different ways. In many households both the husband and wife have to work to make ends meet. A recession puts a huge burden on the growing number of single parents. How do you make enough money to take care of your family? You can work more, hold two jobs. But what does that do to your life? It cuts back on the time that you have for relaxation and for your family.

Where, then, do you get the strength to face tomorrow? When you don't have time to spend with your family and share the love which rejuvenates, this increases the stress and makes life seem all the more difficult.

Women as Priests

There was a time when neither the Catholic church nor the Protestant denominations allowed women to conduct the services. At that time there were enough priests and ministers to go around. Today there is a shortage.

I read recently that for every one hundred priests the Catholic church loses, only fifty-nine come in to replace them. There are fewer students in the seminaries. Why? Some say it's because the Catholic church won't allow women into the priesthood.

Times have changed. Many of the Protestant churches have started to allow women to give the message of God. The stress got so heavy on the ministers that many of them simply burned out. To maintain the church and the religion, they realized that they had to let the women share the responsibility.

The conditions of the times are opening a door for women. A religion or church is not purely for men nor for women. It's for everyone. And this means the family.

Spiritual Training

In ECK, both men and women conduct services. I may conduct the worship service at the ECK Temple myself occasionally. But I also have confidence in other leaders in ECK, men and women, to conduct the services. I have enough pressures and enough other things to do. I am very grateful when someone else can handle it.

Maybe this will be a hint to my colleagues in other religions. Passing around the responsibilities not only gives the ministers a break, it also gives valuable spiritual training to others in the congregation who may help with parts of the service. God's word is not hidden or contained only in the office of the clergy. The word of God is in the heart of each of us.

This is not to say that everybody is equally qualified to speak the message of their religion in front of other people. Speaking before a group is difficult. Some find it to be a terrifying experience. I did in the past, and frankly, I still get edgy. But a speaker who is a bit on the tense side is often more receptive to the audience and responds better to their feelings and needs. So being nervous is not all bad.

Others help bring the message of God in whatever way they feel it themselves. Through music or some other form of the arts, they are using their creative talents to bring upliftment to others.

A Common Thread

ECKANKAR is a worldwide religion with members in almost every country, from just about every religious background, including Buddhism, Hinduism, and all the others. In the West, most of our members were raised in a Christian culture, and the majority were in Christianity at one time or another in their lives.

ECKANKAR has points in common with many other religions. At the core of our teachings is the Light and Sound of God. References to the Light and Sound appear in the Bible in many different forms. For instance, John spoke of it in John 1:1–4 when he said:

In the beginning was the Word, and the Word was with God, and the Word was God.

2 The same was in the beginning with God.

3 All things were made by him; and without him was not any thing made that was made.

4 In him was life; and the life was the light of men.

The word *men* includes women, children, dogs, cats, elephants, and all life, because the light that exists within all living creatures is Soul. The Word is the Voice of God, speaking to Its creations. In ECK we speak of God as IT instead of he or she. God exists, creation exists, and we live in creation.

138

Appearances of the Holy Spirit

How does God speak to us? God speaks through the Holy Spirit. The Holy Spirit is the Word, the Voice of God, which manifests as Light and Sound.

There is a difference between what the Holy Spirit is and the forms in which It may appear. One example is the biblical story of Moses. One day he was tending his father-in-law's flocks out near the end of the desert. When he came to Mt. Horeb, all of a sudden he saw a bush burst into flames. The curious thing was, the bush was not consumed by the fire.

Moses, wanting to see how the bush could catch fire but not burn, went over for a closer look. At first the Bible says that the angel of the Lord appeared in the burning bush. But when Moses got closer, it says, he heard God's Voice speaking from the bush. This angel of the Lord was the form in which the Holy Spirit appeared to Moses.

The Old Testament makes very few references to the Holy Spirit, or the Holy Ghost. There is some mention of It in the story of creation as told in Genesis, as well as in Psalms and the book of Ezekiel. Most references to the Holy Spirit in the purer form come up in the New Testament. Why is this? The people who lived in the times of the Old Testament probably had not yet reached a high enough degree of consciousness to recognize the Holy Spirit.

Yes, it's true that God is, and the Holy Spirit is. But this divine essence, together and one, is recognizable to the human consciousness only through Its aspects, the Light and Sound. How can you divide a person from his voice? Well, the voice is an aspect of the person.

But just because this divine principle exists does not mean that people knew about It, recognized Its aspects, or understood how It spoke to them. Moses saw a burning bush, heard God talking to him, and he was curious.

Word of God

God said, "I've got a little job for you, Moses. You left Egypt some time ago because you killed somebody over there and the police were looking for you. But don't worry, they're all dead. Everybody who might remember the incident is gone."

Then God said, "I want you to talk to Pharaoh, the great ruler of the land. Give him a little message from me. Tell him, 'Oh, by the way, we want to take all the servants, the children of Israel, and just leave. It's going to disrupt your economy a little bit; you won't have any more farm labor to do the dirty work that the Egyptians don't want to do. But God told me that I had to take them out of here.' "

Moses did as he was told. You know how Pharaoh felt about that. But the point is, through the burning bush, God gave Moses the order to go free the children of Israel.

Again, the Word of God comes to us through the two aspects of the Holy Spirit, the Light and Sound. This was an example of both. The burning bush was a form of the Light, and what Moses heard as God's Voice was a form of the Sound.

Pharaoh's resistance brought all kinds of bad things upon the Egyptians—pestilence, plague, and so on. Finally he said, "These people are causing me a lot of problems." The children of Israel then left the land of Egypt, and during their exodus, the Holy Spirit showed up again to lead them.

Old Consciousness

Often people ask the question Why did God have Moses lead the children of Israel around in the wilderness for forty years? Why didn't they just go straight to the land of Canaan, where they settled later?

Some feel it's because the children of Israel might not have had it so bad in Egypt. But they had complained about it, and this is why God said to Moses, "I have heard the cries of my people, and now I'm going to let them go free from Egypt."

But there were practical considerations too. Maybe God knew that as soon as the children of Israel got a few steps away from home, they'd want to go back. "Are you kidding me?" they'd say. "Out here there's no water, no food. And can you believe the heat? I'm going back. It was bad back there, but this is worse."

God had Moses lead the children of Israel straight out to the wilderness while their spirits were still high from their liberation. It was too far to go back to Egypt, so they wandered around out there for forty years.

Why? Probably so that the old generation could die off. What really died out there was the old consciousness of the people who knew what life was like back in Egypt. Though the biblical records cite those who lived for 969 years, like Methuselah, the lifespan had decreased by Moses' time. Some lived a couple hundred years, but most did not.

Pillar of Light

During the forty years in the wilderness, those who had been adults at the time of the exodus, who held on to the old way of thinking, who remembered what life was like back in Egypt, died. Only then could the children of Israel successfully conquer the new land that they were going to take for themselves.

The Light appeared again during the exodus, as described in Exodus, chapter 13:

> 21 And the Lord went before them by day in a pillar of a cloud, to lead them the way; and by night in a pillar of fire, to give them light; to go by day and night:

> 22 He took not away the pillar of the cloud by day, nor the pillar of fire by night, from before the people.

This pillar was an emblem of the Holy Spirit in visible form. Whenever the Holy Spirit appears in some way that we can see, in a form that depends upon light for us to recognize it, this is God speaking to us through Light. The other, more important, way is through Sound.

In this case, the Light came by day as the pillar of a cloud—a visual thing; people could see it. At night it appeared as a pillar of fire—definitely an aspect of Light.

Like a Dove

Another emblem of Light, one of the aspects of the Holy Spirit or the Voice of God, was at the baptism of Jesus in Matthew, chapter 3:

> 16 And Jesus, when he was baptized, went up straightway out of the water: and, lo, the heavens were opened unto him, and he saw the Spirit of God descending like a dove, and lighting upon him:

You will notice it does not say the Spirit of God *was* a dove, but that it was *like* a dove. The writer used the dove as a simile or an image so that people could make a connection with the great unseen Voice of God. Maybe there was a dove, maybe not. Either way, a dove is not the Holy Spirit in Its entirety, but it is one of the ways that the Holy Spirit may show Itself to people.

As a Rushing Wind

A further example of the appearance of the Holy Spirit took place on Pentecost, which is the fiftieth day after Easter. It's from Acts, chapter 2, verses 1 through 4.

And when the day of Pentecost was fully come, they were all with one accord in one place.

2 And suddenly there came a sound from heaven as of a rushing mighty wind [notice it says *as* of a rushing mighty wind—again, a simile], and it filled all the house where they were sitting.

3 And there appeared unto them cloven tongues, like as of fire [another simile], and it sat upon each of them.

4 And they were all filled with the Holy Ghost, and began to speak with other tongues, as the Spirit gave them utterance.

Bridge

These passages can be a bridge between the Christian teachings and the teachings of ECK. They illustrate some of the many ways in which God speaks to us. Although these examples are fairly dramatic, sometimes the Voice of God comes in such commonplace ways that we take It for granted.

We want to make a connection between ourselves here on earth and God above, however you see this. A way to do this is with the sound of HU. HU is another name for

143

God, and HU opens your heart to the Light and Sound of God, which in turn brings love.

Learning Love

It's interesting that whenever people are in the throes of strong emotion—either great pain or happiness—they often sing, play music, or recite poetry. Poetry, of course, is the language of lovers. Why? Because love lifts them beyond their normal state and puts them into a higher state. When you're in love, you're often just blindly, foolishly in love—and may you be so lucky.

Human love is an aspect of divine love. To learn divine love, we must first learn to give love to others here on earth—our family, our mate, our children. This is how we express love.

What is the connection between the Light and Sound and us down here? It's living love. Because God is love, the Holy Spirit, or the ECK, is love. So we, with a purified consciousness as Soul, must also want to live a life that is directed by love. The whole purpose of any religion or church should be to show its people how to love.

There are spiritual exercises that help. Every religion has given some way for its people to find love. Sometimes it's through stories of their saints, and other times it's a song of prayer or a song of praise. Something that helps us find love.

"Amazing Grace" as a Spiritual Exercise

A couple of years ago, when Garrison Keillor was still doing "A Prairie Home Companion" on radio, I caught one of the final shows. As I listened to a well-known country-music singer perform "Amazing Grace," I said, "That is so beautiful."

One of the songs we can use as a spiritual exercise is "Amazing Grace." You can hum it to yourself. A song like that, for whatever reason—just the melody by itself—opens your heart to divine love. So in that, a song like "Amazing Grace" can be a spiritual exercise which opens you to love, and you are able to hear God speak to you. You cannot hear God speak to you unless you open your heart to love first.

"Amazing Grace" was written in the eighteenth century by John Newton. He had been the captain of a ship that carried slaves from Africa. The words must have expressed what he felt when he finally had the realization that if he wanted to be free, he could not take other people into captivity. The song was written sometime after he got out of the slave trade.

Attitudes to Avoid

Some of the words, such as "saved a wretch like me," applied very definitely to John Newton when he was in the slave trade. But they don't apply to most people today. The worst attitude a person can have, next to pride, is a negative image of himself. This may sound like a contradiction or a paradox, but it is not. People often try to cover up their true feelings of unworthiness. How? By walking tall, which comes across as pride.

If you want to call anything a sin, pride and thinking of yourself as dirt are the worst. If you accept the image of yourself as a poor, lost Soul, damned and doomed, then what is the purpose of this life? Just to endure?

With the help of my wife I adapted some of the lyrics of "Amazing Grace" for ECK use. The ECK version is called "Amazing HU."

HU is a name for God that so far has remained unscathed. It is not associated with any of the profanities used to damn something. Just about every language in Christendom has found a way to use God's name to curse somebody. This is not exactly in the spirit of love.

Rewriting the Song

The words, "Amazing grace, how sweet the sound that saved a wretch like me," have been changed to "Amazing HU, how sweet the Sound, that touched a Soul like me."

Another line was, " 'Twas grace that taught my heart to fear." Why make a bad case worse? The words carry a certain philosophy that puts a terrible burden on people which I don't feel is justified.

In the ECK version the words are, " 'Twas HU that taught my heart to sing, and HU my fears relieved." The message of ECK speaks about the Light and Sound of God as the voice of love. Love and fear cannot exist together. If you let love into your heart, it will always drive out fear.

One of the lines in the original version is, "The earth shall soon dissolve like snow." Even Christ said, "There be some standing here, which shall not taste of death, till they see the kingdom of God." After he died, his disciples and others misinterpreted these words to mean that the end of the world was coming soon.

Centuries later, there were people who felt very strongly that the end would come at the millennium in A.D. 1000. The same prediction is being made today as we approach A.D. 2000. I guess they figure God likes a year with round numbers. Others, unwilling to wait for a round number, just pick a certain year and say, "God told me that the end of the world is coming on that date." They've all been wrong so far, haven't they?

A curious line at the end of the original version is, "But God, who called me here below, will be forever mine." This possessiveness is so characteristic of human nature. We are always trying to possess something; we are so good at that. Some see a pretty butterfly and immediately want to catch it and add it to their collection. Or they see a pretty flower growing and have to cut it off and bring it home.

Many people do the same thing when they become passionate about their religion. Like anything else they find pretty or uplifting, they want to capture it and put it on display. To say that God "will be forever mine"— implying that I own God, I possess God—certainly takes a lot of cheek. This concept is no longer appropriate for people today who want to unfold spiritually and find love.

This hymn has a life of its own. One of the verses was added later by someone other than John Newton, and some of the words were revised over the years to fit the changing states of consciousness.

A Prayer to God

This song is also a prayer to God that will open your heart to love. Because until your heart is opened to love, you cannot hear God speak.

I've asked my wife, Joan, accompanied by Bettine Clemen, to sing this song at today's service.

Amazing HU

(The ECK version of "Amazing Grace")*

Amazing HU, how sweet the Sound,
That touched a Soul like me!
I once was lost, but now am found,
Was blind, but now I see.

147

'Twas HU that taught my heart to sing,
And HU my fears relieved;
How precious did HU then appear
The hour I first believed!

Through many dangers, toils, and snares,
I have already come;
'Tis HU has brought me safe thus far,
And HU will lead me home.

The HU has given life to me,
Its Sound my hope secures;
My shield and portion HU will be
As long as life endures.

The earth will someday pass away;
The sun forbear to shine;
But God, who sent me here below,
I'll be forever Thine.

You may want to sing this song or even just hum the melody to yourself whenever you feel troubled. By thinking of HU or an uplifting melody such as this, you are saying to God, "Please show me thy ways. Please lead me to truth."

ECK Worship Service, Temple of ECK, Chanhassen, Minnesota, May 5, 1991

---

* *Lyrics adapted by Joan and Harold Klemp from the public-domain song "Amazing Grace" by John Newton (1725–1807). Sung with the traditional American melody for "Amazing Grace."*

I taught my daughter how to play ball. I wanted to teach her how to do a very few things but do them well.

12

Keys to the Spiritual Life

Why should anyone turn to religion in the nineties? From my position as a spiritual leader, you would think I would say, "Everybody needs a spiritual life." That everyone should get into a religious organization.

But sometimes I wonder why anybody gets into religion—simply because most religions are not in touch with the needs of people.

This is who I'm trying to bring the teachings of ECK to through the outer structure of ECKANKAR. I'm trying to make ECKANKAR responsive to the spiritual needs of people. But many leaders in ECK were leaders in other religions. And I find they have brought with them so many of the things that prevent people from making a connection with the necessary parts of the spiritual life— although they're doing their very best.

Love Is Essential

What are the necessary parts of the spiritual life?

First of all, that a person love something or someone more than themselves. This is absolutely essential.

How do you think people can maximize their lives?

To get anywhere spiritually, you have to love what you're doing. If you love what you're doing, then you're going to do the very best at whatever you do. That's what people should do if they want to live a spiritual life.

When I say do the very best at whatever you do, I'm talking about things that build. I'm not talking about destructive things, of course. To love what you do and do the very best you can is the bottom line to me.

So many people today just get by. People make fun of the Protestant work ethic, but that's too bad because we've replaced it with reliance on government welfare systems. This means even if we could work, we don't. I think people are cheating themselves when they expect someone else to solve their problems for them.

Responsibility

How important is it to take an active role in managing your own life and taking responsibility for living your life? My mother said she joined ECKANKAR because she heard you did your own grocery shopping. She didn't think the pope would do that.

Taking responsibility is very important. As a small example, I do shop for my own groceries. I read labels. Sometimes people see me in the store, and if they aren't dressed as neatly as they feel they should be, they don't come up to say hello. They just think, "There's the spiritual leader of ECKANKAR over there reading labels." But the ECK, Divine Spirit, does something to make us eventually bump into each other and say hi.

I think we should take the best science has to offer today and the best Spirit has to offer, put the two together, and find a happy combination. If we find it, I think we can make ourselves happier people.

Human Experiences

Who do you admire as a philosopher, writer, actor, or businessperson?

I've always admired Mark Twain. I've read most everything published on him. He could see through what people took so seriously about themselves. He had this very nice way of turning a phrase and making people laugh at themselves.

We human beings take ourselves so seriously. We finally see that we are actually pretty ridiculous in some of the things we do.

I try to remind myself not to take myself too seriously. Sometimes the weight and responsibilities of my position as a leader become heavy. People think, "You're a spiritual leader; you don't have to deal with stress." But I have my concerns too, where I have to learn to deal with stress.

You said earlier that your mother got into ECKANKAR because she came to a seminar and heard me say that I do my own grocery shopping. She thought the pope was not about to go out and do his own shopping. But maybe he can't; everyone knows him in town. Not too many people know me, so I can walk around and do this.

But unlike the pope, I know some things about human relations, being married, and having children, that he could never know. There are some things about being married, having a child, and getting married again, that you don't find in a book.

You cannot give people spiritual direction unless you've had certain experiences yourself. Anyone who's been married will know what I'm saying about marriage; someone who hasn't been married, won't. Anyone who's been married but hasn't had children won't understand exactly what I'm saying about having a child. Those who have had at least one child will understand what I'm saying. Then there's a whole world of people who have had more than one child; they know more than what I'm saying.

Relieving Stress

How do you alleviate stress in your life?

I always try to orient everything to my mission—to let people know about ECK in some way. I have two outlets. One is talking with people on computer bulletin boards. I talk with them about religion, ethics, and other issues.

I meet very interesting people—agnostics, people who are strong in religion, people who are very quick of mind, people who have real concerns about the spiritual life. I talk with them.

The other outlet is video games.

What are your favorites?

I've played Top Landing a few times. It's impressive. It's a realistic video game where you are the captain of a jumbo jet coming in for a landing or trying to take off. It's hard enough to get to the runway. The game is made in Japan, so you land in places like Osaka or Sydney, Australia.

The video graphics are very good. It's very realistic, nothing dramatic. If you're on target, the ECK will bring a spiritual principle; if you're not, the little gauge tells you. It tells you what the crosswind is.

We have crosswinds in our lives all the time. When we're landing, we can come down too fast. If we go down too fast, we end up short on the runway and we have to come up with two more tokens. Some of these games are very spiritual.

Having a Sense of Humor

How important is having a sense of humor? What makes you laugh?

Sometimes the simplest things make me laugh. I grew up on a farm; I was around animals. But when I got to the city, I felt kind of separated from it.

I began putting out a bird feeder, and all of a sudden birds came. We have two ducks visiting the feeder: Donald and Daisy. I put food in a little dish on the ground for them. Donald is a noble duck; Daisy just goes after the food. She stuffs herself full and then moves toward the other dish.

She's kind of a selfish duck. When she's done she waddles off toward the road where they have their landing pad. Poor Donald hasn't even eaten, but she's done. Donald takes one look at the dish, grabs a bite, then runs for the girl. To me, this is one of the funny things in life.

They're so much like people. One person in a relationship will always be going faster than the other.

I also like Laurel and Hardy. It's along the lines of Mark Twain—poking fun at the pretenses of the human race. One of the pair does everything pompously, the other with comical effect. He makes a bad problem worse until it can't get any worse. Then the whole thing blows up, and the story ends on a high note.

Why We're Here

So you feel that certain fundamental principles of life can be seen in things we might consider mundane?

Very much in the mundane. We have more people living on earth than ever before. We're getting crowded. We have too many chickens in the chicken coop. In a crowded space, we begin to peck away at each other. We draw blood. Why? Because we're basically unhappy.

When people are unhappy, they're always attacking others. Unless we make greater efforts than ever before, we're going to have more problems as the world becomes more crowded.

When the Berlin Wall came down, everyone was saying, "Now we'll have peace." I told everyone in ECK, "Work as hard as you can now and tell people behind the Iron Curtain about the teachings of ECK and what Divine Spirit really is. There's just a short opening now. There will be more war."

Back then, when the wall came down, no one could imagine more war. But a year or so later we had the Gulf War. It's not the end. There will never be peace in this world. People get upset when they hear me say this.

Basically they misunderstand why this world exists. It is not to have peace. This doesn't mean that the people in this world are not to strive for peace. They are. But in striving for peace they are purifying themselves. They are becoming spiritual beings. This is why God sent them here to begin with.

Being Happy

Do you think it's possible for a person to be happy all the time?

On the flight from Minnesota two flight attendants served the meals. One was a tall, easygoing, blonde woman named Erin. Everything was a joke to her because that was her nature.

The other person was more serious and busy. At one point she said to Erin, "If you stack the trays like this, it's a lot easier." Erin said, "Oh, great. Label it a technological advance, right here on the plane." She was laughing a lot. It was just her attitude.

They are just different kinds of people. One person's nature is to be carefree; people like this can't help being like that. The other person is more serious; people like this are just that way. The very happy person can also have many serious and troubling moments and may be laughing to cover them up. The serious person won't always be serious but will also have happy moments.

No matter what your basic character is, you can do a lot to make yourself a happy person by being responsible for what you do in this world and not blaming somebody else for your mistakes.

Self-Confidence

Why does being responsible for what you do make you feel better about yourself or your life?

I taught my daughter how to play ball at five or six. I wanted to show her how to do a very few things but do them well.

She was a timid little kid, and I was pitching the ball at her fast. I got her a bat that was the right size for her, but for the longest time she couldn't even hit anything. I encouraged her. I showed her how to meet the ball with the bat. Finally she learned how to hit.

Once you learn how to be good at a few things it carries over into other areas. Now she's growing up, she just graduated from high school. She has the confidence to go out and take a chance on life.

I find so many people in the world today aren't willing to take a chance because they haven't found out how to do one thing well. Some will expect everyone else to do for them. They live in a fantasy world. They believe they have failed because of society, because they haven't had a good education. I hear this a lot. But blaming others for what you don't have is one of the biggest lies we have in society today.

Work Ethic

We have immigrants coming into the U.S. from Asia. I respect them so much. They realize what you need to get along in this world, what is valuable to the people in a certain society. In the United States we place a high priority on learning and skills that require literacy. So they become literate.

And they don't just become literate to the level that we are used to. They have exceeded us as a group. It's almost as if the earlier groups that came to the U.S. have become lazy. They came here and became established; they set their businesses up the way their fathers did it. Then the third and fourth generations didn't have to work so hard. They lived on Grandpa's money, inventiveness, and sweat of the brow.

The Vietnamese are using the inventiveness and sweat of the brow that our great-grandparents had. We've been living off the fat of the land. And I find there's a lot of unhappiness in this land of plenty. The immigrants who are coming to our country are bringing new life. They are restoring the work ethic.

The work ethic has nothing to do with religion. It's when someone or a group of people believe that if you're on this earth you need to work to survive. By being able to do one thing well, you become a very self-reliant, self-confident person.

Touching God

Does doing one thing well put you in touch with a deeper, more spiritual side of yourself?

I think this deeper, spiritual side of oneself expresses itself as happiness and confidence. When it comes out at least a little each day, you've touched the Higher Self. You've touched God.

This is how God speaks to people. So many times we hear people who speak of the Holy Spirit say, "I know God is in my life." But often it's a pretty dreary life; they don't have anybody.

One day I came out of a video arcade in a big shopping center. A middle-aged woman was walking by, and for some reason we caught each other's eye. I said, "Do you ever go in there?" "Me? Oh, no," she said, like I'd just come out of some gambling den. I thought, "How sad that this woman has stopped growing, stopped living."

She doesn't realize that the real education of our youth is happening on computers and in video arcades.

When we got into the Gulf War, it was this younger generation who knew how to use the modern technology. It's one thing for a few top scientists to develop weapons or even technology to build constructively in society, but if no one in the society has the training or consciousness to use the technology, how long is it going to work?

If you want to know how a society can fall in on itself,

159

travel to where the Iron Curtain used to be. Stay in the hotels there. You'll find out how service to one's fellow beings can fall to such a low level. There is incredible air pollution in East Germany and Poland; it's literally hell on earth, like living under a volcano.

This is not a natural catastrophe; it's man-made. It's a reflection of the consciousness of the people who came together to set up their own government. It was a Communist form of government, something which is as dead as the countries are now, both economically and spiritually.

This is why there is a need for the spiritual works in the world today, to understand how the Holy Spirit works. The orthodox religions have forgotten how God makes a connection with people in their everyday lives.

Loving Yourself

God speaks through you. God speaks through your neighbor to you. This is why Christ said to love your neighbor as yourself. In Christianity today there is so much self-hate. I think it's because of the celibacy in the Christian church that wasn't there in the beginning.

Celibacy came in later. For some people it's very natural to be celibate. But I feel the reason the Christian church went wrong was they felt lovemaking was dirty. Saint Paul in Corinthians said something like this: If you can't contain yourself, then it's OK to get married. It was like marriage was OK if you couldn't be "Godlike" enough. Read 1 Corinthians, especially chapter 7. I feel Saint Paul missed the boat.

Every religious group has its fringe ideas. Celibacy was one of the fringe ideas of normal, human living that got twisted out of proportion and became a mainstay in the church. I find it interesting that Martin Luther married a former nun. This was almost a happy return to how things were once.

Love is a God-given gift. Love between man and woman is beautiful, and I think the Christian church went wrong by saying sex was dirty.

How can one learn to love?

I'll go back to the statement Christ made, "Love your neighbor as yourself." I think what has happened in the Christian church is there was too little true love of a person for himself. Christ said to love your neighbor as yourself. You have to love yourself first before you can love anybody else. This is where everything begins.

Life Changes

The church has not been able to teach people how to love. So now the burden falls upon me as the leader of the spiritual teachings of ECK. What do I say? First you have to make this connection with the Voice of God, because God is love. How do you do it? By singing HU.

HU is a name for God that most people don't know. Singing HU begins to open a person's heart to the divine reality, to God. I'm speaking of divine love, true love— not celibacy and all the other kinds of love which are mistaken for true love.

When you open your heart to love, your life begins to change. But it seldom changes the way you expect it to, or even the way you want it to. We have our own opinions of what our lives should be, but if we are off the path to God and don't know it, we are setting up our lives to go a certain direction. Then God puts us back on the path, and we take a new direction. It's going to break up all the expectations that we had in the past of what our lives should be.

When people come to ECK, they sometimes find their lives speed up. Life becomes more adventurous and exciting. Sometimes they say, "Please, I don't want any more excitement." But if you let it, your life will move progressively forward. And it all begins with the singing of HU.

What Is Success

What would you say success is?

We've seen rich, unhappy people and rich, happy people. We've seen poor, unhappy people and poor, happy people. So we know that success has nothing to do with money. But today in our society many people are getting into lawsuits; they feel it's the quick way to get money.

A couple of centuries ago, certain rare tulips used to be worth a fortune. People sold everything they had, even their tools to make a living, just to get a certain tulip. People said, "Tulips are it," and they gave a false value to them just as we give a false value to money today.

A cobbler in Holland, as the story goes, had thus acquired a very rare black tulip. Some merchants came to him and said, "We would like to buy that black tulip." Although it was priceless, he said OK and sold it for what today would be equivalent to a few hundred dollars, a very small amount.

He took his money and gave the tulip bulb to one of the merchants. Immediately the man put the bulb on the ground and smashed it with his foot. The cobbler was stunned. The man said, "We would have paid you a fortune for that bulb that you gave away for practically nothing. We already have a black tulip, and you would have been competition."

The cobbler had lost everything except the money he now had and the memory of having given away a fortune for a crushed tulip. It was a devastating story.

People are doing that today. They get into lawsuits and think if they can just earn a huge amount of money, they'll be happy. It's a trick of life. It says, "Yes, you can have this money, and if you're very smart in a couple of years we'll let you file another lawsuit and get another large amount of money."

But what the person doesn't realize is that he has a spiritual defect in character. That defect will go with this person through this life into the next life. Someday, life will say, "OK, the game's over. Now you pay." And the payment will be in the true coin. All the money or tulip bulbs a person has accrued won't be enough to stave off the debt that's come due. Because the debt won't be able to be paid back in money.

The person will experience some disease or emotional heartbreak that no amount of money can fix. I think this is what people don't understand. This is what earth is for: for people to learn how to become more Godlike beings. But they think life on earth is for all these other things, like becoming rich.

To become rich they do something selfish and step on things, then they say, "I am correcting something that seems to have gone wrong." By doing this, they destroy. They feel they have done something creative, but they can't do an act of love by destroying something else.

Power or True Love?

True responsibility is recognizing the difference between acting on power and acting on love. People who act on true love always build. They will never do something that destroys anything else. People who act for power say, "I will build a city. I will build this great monument as a tribute to mankind, to my own greatness." But if anything is built on power, it generally has to destroy something in this world to come into manifestation.

So few people recognize the difference between power and love. There will always be power. This is why, if you can find love, do. Love between man and woman is the most grateful release.

Today something else is coming into the mainstream: love between two people of the same gender. Right away all of the moralists become upset. "This is not right," they say. Who are these people to speak for God's will?

I usually find this kind of person very intolerant. They're always trying to censor the freedom of other people's consciousness. They are always out there, busy minding other people's business.

To me, love between two women or two men is as valid as love between a man and a woman. The important thing is to love someone or something outside of yourself.

Some youth came to me once and put me on the spot. They asked me, "Why do the ECK Masters say that youth should retain their virginity?" My feeling is this: any relationship between responsible adults that is done in love—whether or not it is sanctified by some country or organization or religion—is a marriage. I'm not talking about people who are minors, who often try to make believe they are grown up, that they have a deep abiding love like Romeo and Juliet. This often turns out to be infatuation.

Humility

How important is humility?

A person who has truly learned to love is a humble person. But this person will not wear humility like a

164

badge on the shoulder. In fact, a person who is humble often doesn't know he is humble.

Humility is a natural offshoot of a person who truly has love for himself or herself. This love also translates into a love for other people. Usually people who love other people are humble.

A humble person is someone who can laugh at himself and with others. Humility is seeing the goodness in other people.

The Five Passions

How detrimental are the five passions of the mind?

They're always with us in some degree in our everyday lives. All we can hope to do is control them. You might wonder, "Do you control them by force of will?" No, by loving more.

Each one of these five passions—anger, attachment, lust, greed, and vanity—will come to the forefront in your life at some time. You may want a parking spot, and someone else pulls into it in front of you. All the frustrations you had that morning suddenly vent themselves, and you lean on your horn.

At this particular moment, anger is very bad for you. It's letting loose a lot of things inside you that are not good for your health. People don't realize that a life of anger causes disease. They don't know this because they can't trace the cause and effect very clearly. There is always a connection between what they do and what they are, but people don't realize that sometimes.

When someone pulls into your parking spot, you get angry and then blame the anger on the other person. This is not taking responsibility for yourself. First of all, if you really did love the other person, you would sit there and say, "He wants it worse than I did; there will be another parking spot," and you let the situation be. Or maybe you would realize that the parking spot is for a small car. And you think, "Thank God I didn't park in that spot. I'll go find a larger parking spot."

Suffering and Learning

Do you think it's possible to learn without suffering?

Absolutely not. But here's the distinction I make: Some people make suffering a life mission. People used to wear hairshirts or become celibate not because it was their natural inclination but because they thought it would make God love them. I feel that when suffering comes to pass in this life—which it does—it's life trying to teach us something.

There's an old saying that every cloud has a silver lining. When a cloud comes into your life, look for the silver lining because it's there. If you can't see what the silver lining in the cloud is, sing HU. This will open your heart so you can say, "Thy will be done."

Attitude of Love

This is the real meaning of the word *HU*. It's adopting the attitude: not my will, but thy will.

You'd be surprised at how few people have this attitude. It shows up in their prayers. When they pray to God, they tell God what to do. They tell God exactly how much money they want or how they have a certain problem with a receding hairline. They ask God to fix it. If God doesn't and their whole emotional being gets tied up in the receding hairline, they'll be a mess as they get older and lose more hair.

166

If you pray to God, be thankful for the gift of life. Thank God for that, then go on and handle the rest of your life as best you can.

I have a cousin who when he was four wanted to live forever. When he was twelve he said the meaning of life is true profound psychological stability. What do you think the meaning of life is?

This kid is intellectually profound, but I wouldn't guarantee he'll live a happy life. He is making something that is very simple, very complicated. People who have a very intricate mind system can't help putting a labyrinth of words to how they feel and what their goals in life are.

If someone said to me, "I would like to learn to love all life," this would be the greatest thing a person could live for. This is the whole purpose of this life—to love God truly.

Spiritual Strength

What do you think builds strength in a person?

Suffering could build strength, but only if a person acknowledges his or her responsibility for whatever went wrong.

Sometimes you can't. Sometimes what goes wrong in this life is caused by something you did in your last lifetime. If you don't remember, you're not able to connect cause and effect.

I talk about health so much because when something goes wrong in this area, you can watch what you eat and many times find out how to correct it. There is often a closer cause and effect there.

How do you know when you're getting stronger? Other people can often tell better than you, yourself. A humble person wouldn't even put attention on that because it's inside yourself. The only way you really know if you're stronger is if you go through a time of hardship and you get through it somehow by listening. You trust something inside yourself—the strength you have gained to this point.

Surrender to the Right Principle

There's a funny thing about suffering: You're usually put at the mercy of life where you have to trust someone else, whether they're a medical person or a financial company helping you out of a crisis. You have to surrender and let go. This is another element of the ECK teachings—to give up and let go. But you have to give up and let go to the right thing.

The right thing to give up to is the creative principle, God. In other words, you say, "I want something better in my life." For instance, your debts have caught up with you and you have to go to an accountant. When you come to the accountant, you're basically saying, "I give up."

A person who goes to an accountant for help with the debts that are piling up is no different than someone who goes to a clergyperson saying, "My life is so hard. Help me." They're both a form of surrender.

How much help you get at this point depends on the competence of the accountant or the clergyperson. In every field there are different levels of competence.

I know the printing field. In printing you can spend a lot for a bad printer, and you can spend less money for a good one. You can spend a lot on a bad plumbing job, or you can spend the same or less and get good work done. It comes down to the person you work with. How

168

do you find someone who is going to help you find your way to a better life? It's trial and error.

I offer the word *HU*. If HU helps you overcome some problem in your life—where you get understanding to go to the right people for help—you may be ready to know about the teachings of ECK. This will be your next connection with the secret teachings.

I call them secret, not because they're secret out here but because they're secret inside each person. Christ said, "The kingdom of God is within you." He was speaking about a state of consciousness, the kingdom of heaven within people.

Find that and all things shall be added unto you, he said. Find this kingdom of love. Find this connection. The starting point is HU; it will open your heart. Until your heart is open to love, you haven't begun on the path to God.

Cloak of Consciousness

What is the cloak of consciousness?

The cloak of consciousness is actually the Mahanta. This is the highest state of consciousness that we know about. There will be people who dispute this, who say the Krishna or Christ state of consciousness is higher. But what difference does it make unless you, yourself, have it?

You feel that people continue to evolve. Do you feel that you personally are continually evolving?

Absolutely. This is the plus factor in ECK, the plus factor in life. There is no final state of perfection. We are continually moving either into higher states or backward in consciousness. When you let despondency or greed or

169

other states take over your life, then you are moving down the ladder of life in the wrong direction. You can lose in spiritual consciousness just as you can gain in spiritual consciousness.

Most people of the world are going nowhere in consciousness. They're spiritually dead, at a standstill. They don't know they're treading on the wheel of life, a treadmill that goes nowhere, just like a squirrel running in his cage. He's going around, but he's going nowhere.

Pointing the Way Out

What advice would you give to those people?

What do you suggest to people who aren't aware of their condition? If you tell them about it, they're going to argue with you. As I said, people defend the Christ consciousness even though they don't have any idea of what it is. If I talk to these people and tell them, "You don't have the consciousness," they would just want to fight with me. What are they fighting about?

If a person has something in his or her life, it's there. You don't have to tell them about it. They see it. My job is basically to go out and tell people about the Light and Sound of God and how to make a connection with It. It is the Voice of God, the Holy Spirit.

And how do you make this connection? With HU. You sing this song, this ancient song of HU.

And when you start, you may become aware of the limits of your consciousness. Most people aren't. They are in the perfect world of their creation, a little box. They've made it themselves, with all its limitations, and they feel it is the final creation, that it's finished. Yet they're unhappy in it, and they don't know where to go. They don't know there's a skylight and a trapdoor that leads to the skylight. If you suggest there is a way out, they become very angry with you. Unless they're willing to make a change in their own lives, I as a spiritual leader cannot help them.

I work in the capacity of the Inner and Outer Master. As the Outer Master I give people the outer teachings. I can tell them about the books of ECKANKAR and how the books can help them start to see the secret teachings. As the Inner Master I come to them in the dream state. I talk to them and meet with them. Gradually they become aware of the secret, inner teachings, through the dream state. Then I can begin showing them there's more to life than they could ever have imagined.

Solomon said, "There is no new thing under the sun." He was right. What I'm trying to show people is there is life beyond the sun.

Toward Self-Responsibility

For people who may not feel ready for ECKANKAR, are there other steps? Some people talk about Alcoholics Anonymous as a step. Are there other places you would send people to?

All these groups help people to be more responsible than they have been in the past. In this way these organizations are good for people, but they're elementary steps to the path of ECK. They're basically teaching people to look at themselves and the lives they live, that their state of consciousness could be better than it is.

It's better than lying in the gutter as a drunk. The only time Alcoholics Anonymous can help a person is if he says, "You're right. It's cold and dirty in the gutter here. I want something better." Until the person says, "I want something better," no one can help him or her.

171

There are many good organizations like this. The Christian religion is good for people; the Hindu religion is good for people; the Edgar Cayce group is good for certain people. They are all part of the divine plan. God has put them all here so that people can evolve spiritually along the path which provides the least resistance to them.

This is why there should be less animosity between these groups. God established the Islamic religion just as he established the Christian religion, but he also established ECKANKAR. Each of these religions is valid.

So what's important is that the group lead you toward self-responsibility?

Exactly. Those groups are part of the divine plan for bringing Souls to a higher level of spiritual awareness.

Private Interview, Anaheim, California,
June 21, 1991

172

I realized that it was a duck, gliding along in the left lane like a commuter. People do a lot of strange things, but this incident made me realize that ducks do strange things too.

13

Ducks Do Strange Things Too!

A couple of years ago, shortly after I moved to Minnesota, I was driving along the freeway. There were several lanes of traffic going in my direction. All of a sudden I noticed something strange over a car ahead of me. Naturally I was curious, so I drove a little faster to catch up.

Goose in the Fast Lane

As I got closer, I saw that it was a large Canada goose flying about a foot above a car in the fast lane.

Somebody must have befriended it when it was just a little gosling, I thought. Maybe they kept it in the garage along with the family car, so this goose had imprinted on cars. For whatever reason, it had picked out that particular vehicle to fly over.

I watched fascinated as it stayed just a wing beat above the roof of the car. It seemed very pleased with itself as it kept pace with the flow of traffic.

At the time I just thought, This is Minnesota. But as the months passed and I didn't see a whole lot more of that, I realized it actually was unusual even for Minnesota. Or so I thought.

Ducks Do Strange Things Too!

About two months ago, I left a grocery store and had just pulled out onto a four-lane street. Traffic was light in the two lanes coming toward me.

Two blocks down on the opposite side of the street, I saw something just above the level of the pavement. When it got closer, I realized that it was a duck, gliding along in the left lane like a commuter. I also noticed that he was flying faster than the speed limit. His unswerving sense of purpose made me wonder, "Does he go home this way every night?"

I turned my head to watch as he flew past my car, staying just about two feet above the pavement. Then I looked in the mirror to see where he would go. Except for the goose, it was the strangest thing I'd ever seen.

The duck then changed lanes, and he didn't even signal. About a block ahead of him was a traffic light. For the sake of the duck and the other vehicles, I hoped the light would be green when he got to it. If he didn't know how to obey a simple traffic law like signaling a lane change, he surely wouldn't know how to stop for a red light. I was worried that he would hit someone. But he flew out of my view, so I don't know what happened.

People do a lot of strange things, but this incident made me realize that ducks do strange things too. This particular bird broke a lot of traffic laws—he was speeding, he didn't signal a lane change, and he probably ran the red light at the next intersection. On the other hand, he was flying on the proper side of the road, so maybe he wasn't that dumb after all.

Donald and Daisy

There are two ducks that visit us regularly at home. We call them Donald and Daisy. Donald is a real gentleman, a very fine duck. And though I don't like to say it, Daisy is a little selfish.

The two ducks fly in every night right at sundown, then stand out on the lawn and quack to signal their arrival. That means that I'd better get busy and put the birdseed out there, so I open the garage door and hustle out to the backyard.

One day I moved the dish from the front yard to the back, and they got lost. Not knowing how else to communicate with them, I had to go "cluck, cluck, cluck" until they finally figured out that I was trying to lead them to the food dish in the backyard. Between the clucking and the two wild birds waddling behind me on the lawn, the neighbors must have thought we were three pretty strange ducks.

The Noble Duck

I always put seed in one dish and water in another so they can have something to drink with their food. Daisy positions herself right between the two dishes. She eats seed, drinks water, eats seed, drinks water—back and forth until she's full. Donald stretches his neck as high as he can and nobly stands guard.

At that point I go back inside the house to prevent the mosquitoes from enjoying me for their dinner. I watch from the window.

When Daisy has had her fill, does she wait for Donald to take his turn? No. She immediately turns and waddles up the little hill on our lawn, heading straight to their landing pad on the road. From there she takes right off and flies home.

Donald would like to stay and eat, but he's too kind. He looks at the dish, then at his beloved Daisy waddling away, and he gallantly follows her up to the road. He hasn't had a thing to eat yet, and I feel so sorry for him.

One day I told my wife, "You know, Donald really is a noble duck."

"You don't hear that too often," she said.

Donald's not stupid, either. One evening he arrived on schedule and quacked loudly to make sure I heard him. When he's really hungry, he'll leave Daisy and come alone to get his own meal. But instead of coming straight to my lawn, he'll land on the roof next door.

Nothing looks more ridiculous than a duck sitting on top of a house. They should swim in the water or walk on land, but they should not sit on top of a house. It doesn't look right.

Donald stays up there long enough to look around very carefully. When the coast is clear, he comes sailing over to my lawn, eats his dinner, and then flies home to Daisy.

Troublesome People

A friend of mine is an amateur magician. He told me that he always carries one or two little tricks with him, mostly as a defense against brattish children. Very firm with his own children, he can't understand why other parents won't discipline theirs when they act up in restaurants and other public places.

Occasionally an unruly child will come over to him and do things to annoy him. He can't say anything, of course, because the parents are right there.

Over dinner he showed us how he deals with these kids. Pulling a red handkerchief from his pocket, he said, "Do you want to see this disappear?"

"Sure," we said.

He balled up the handkerchief, and by skillful sleight of hand, he made it disappear. Then he made it reappear. He was very good.

178

He said, "Whenever a child comes up to me and acts bratty, I show him this trick. Then I tell him, 'If you don't behave, I'll make you disappear too.' The kid is usually so awestruck that he goes back to his parents and leaves me alone."

I think of doing this sometimes, too, when I have to deal with people who act like strange ducks. But in my position, I can't pull a handkerchief from my pocket and say, "Be good or I'll make you disappear." I have to work indirectly, speaking to troublesome people as if they were spiritual adults who can hear what I'm saying.

The message I try to get across to them, whether they hear it or not, is this: It's time to act like a grownup. Nobody pays attention to you when you act like a spoiled brat. You think you'll be happy if you scream and raise a fuss until somebody notices you. It doesn't work that way; you won't be happy.

They don't believe me, of course. I spend a certain amount of time speaking with them as one spiritual being to another, but if I can't get through, I don't fight with them. When I've tried my best to make a situation work out and I'm not able to, I just wash my hands of it. I turn it over to the ECK; I let it go completely. All the events that have begun their play must now run their course.

Practicing Spiritual Maturity

Time and again I have observed that people who engage in any kind of spiritual blackmail are carrying around an emotional problem. They are convinced that they are acting on behalf of a divine cause. But their conduct makes things worse instead of better.

Ironically, in the process of exposing a situation they don't like, they also expose something about their own life. It always works both ways, equally and fairly.

179

Many who study the ECK teachings say they understand the principle of love and spiritual maturity. Yet when it comes down to actually practicing it in their daily lives, some of them have absolutely no idea what the spiritual laws of ECK are all about.

I do what I can to counsel people. I often tell them outright, "The defects you see are those you created in the past and brought into this lifetime yourself. The problems you see in others are your own problems. You're pointing the finger in the wrong direction."

Character Defects

I have spoken of this at seminars many times. Everybody nods as if they understand. But as soon as the talk is over, many go out and break the same spiritual laws again.

Their understanding lasts only until something comes up in their life that crosses them. It stirs their emotions and makes them angry, so they strike out at someone else. It doesn't occur to them to be quiet, go into contemplation, and ask the Mahanta, the true Inner Master, "Let me see thy ways. Let me see thy truth. Let me see with love."

Instead, they think that somehow they are not going against the ECK. They do not realize that merely believing that does not make it so. One must be absolutely sure that what he is doing is truly of the ECK and not based solely on the human impulses. Since these are of a lower nature, they can be inaccurate and misleading.

The ECK in Its wisdom is trying to work out these defects in a person's spiritual character. Often this means having to go through suffering and hardship. I have never seen anyone grow substantially who has not gone through a period of suffering or trial.

If you can go through the trials of life and say, "I wonder what ECK is trying to tell me," you will be far richer in consciousness than if you say, "Now who's to blame for this?" Meaning, of course, anyone but you.

Mall Escape

In Minnesota there are a number of very large indoor malls. A couple of weeks ago I was shopping at one. These malls always have a sales and marketing office somewhere near one of the entrances. Periodically, out of the doorway of the office come people with clipboards who remind me of little ducks. The clipboards stick out from under their arm like a patch of feathers, and their head swivels left and right as if they're out looking for birdseed. Sometimes I think they see me as their birdseed.

One day I stood there patiently and let one of those researchers interview me. Very adept at invasion, he asked all kinds of things that I really didn't care to tell him. Finally I just said, "I don't want to answer any more questions."

A few days later another researcher at the same shopping mall stopped me and said, "Could I ask you a few questions? Have you taken our questionnaire?"

"I just took one," I said. This response worked a few times, but then they got smart. They're like the ducks: If you move the seed dish, it doesn't take them long to find the new spot. The last time I said "I took the test already," the person asked, "Oh? What was it about?"

"I don't remember," I said, slowly backing away from her. "It was two or three years ago."

These people take the pleasure out of shopping. They seem to hover near the entrances, waiting to swoop down on you as soon as you come in the door. To avoid them,

181

you have to fight your way through the gauntlet. First you look around to make sure no one is watching you. Then you race to the nearest pillar, flatten your back against it, and hope no one with a clipboard has spotted you.

When you're sure it's safe to go further, you run as fast as you can to the next pillar. Here you stop to catch your breath, wondering if you'll ever make it to the shops. Even if you manage to get to the stores without being caught, you must then follow the same procedure to get out of there.

Parking-Lot Hunt

Two weeks ago I went into the mall, made a mad dash through the gauntlet, did my shopping, and even made my way out of there without being accosted. But when I got to the parking lot, I saw a man in a nice suit roaming among the parked cars with a clipboard in his hand. Oh, no, I thought. Is no place on earth sacred?

Then I noticed the strange look on his face. Suddenly it struck me: That man has lost his car. He isn't looking for victims to interview at all.

He reminded me of a lost Soul in the other worlds. I run into them there; I run into them in parking lots. Trying to act as if he knew where he was going, the man looked important and businesslike as he strode briskly through the rows of cars. But I could tell he wasn't going anywhere in particular.

I lost my car there one time too. This is a very tricky shopping mall. I was pretty sure he had entered a store on the upper level, then came outside on the lower level, and didn't realize his car was in the upper parking lot. He probably thought it had been stolen. I decided to get involved.

It didn't take me long to realize that the best way to catch up with a pedestrian in a parking lot is not with a car. Unlike me, the man wasn't limited to the one-way traffic lanes. Each time he cut through the rows of cars, I would drive around to where he was as fast as I could. Just as I got there, he would turn around and go in the opposite direction, leaving me adrift in that huge parking lot.

Finally I figured out where to head him off. I drove the car over there and rolled down my window. He didn't see me; he was busy looking off in the distance, as a person who has lost his car tends to do.

Being a Co-worker with God

When he came closer, I called out the window, "Could you help me, please?" I thought that would keep him from running away or ignoring me.

"Yes," he said, and came closer.

"Have you lost your car?" I asked.

"Yes," he admitted. He looked very embarrassed.

"I lost my car here once too," I said. "Which entrance did you use when you went into the store?"

"The front door of Penney's."

"The same thing happened to me," I explained. "I didn't realize there were two entrances to Penney's and that they both look exactly the same. One is down here, and the other is on the upper level. Do you see those steps way back there that take you up that hill?" He looked and nodded. I said, "Walk up those steps, and I think you'll find your car."

He was so relieved. Then he looked in my car window and noticed the red gadget on the floor. It was a security device used to lock the steering wheel. "Does that thing work?" he asked.

"I really couldn't tell you," I said. "Every time I come back to my car, it's still there, so I don't know."

I told him how I had lost my car the first time I came to this particular shopping center. It was a cold, rainy night in early fall. I had left Penney's and walked around in the rain for an hour and a half trying to figure out why my car wasn't where I had parked it.

Finally noticing the hill, it dawned on me that I must have parked the car up there. I took a deep breath and climbed the stairs. If I'm going to die of exposure anyway, I thought, it might as well be on a hill.

At the top of the stairs was another big parking lot and an entrance sign that read "J.C. Penney." It was identical to the one downstairs. That's where I found my car, and that's when I got the idea to buy this red steel object. I felt that at least my car would be where I had left it. Hearing my story, which was similar to his own experience, the man who had lost his car got the idea to buy one of those for himself.

So you learn through your own experience. But you can also learn by observing the safeguards taken by another person who has been through the same experience you are having now. In other words, be smart enough to benefit from his experience.

Open Consciousness

How do you do that? You do it with your consciousness. I teach you all kinds of strategies to live this life better. But unless you have the consciousness to perceive what the ECK or the Mahanta is giving you, you will not be able to accept these bits of spiritual wisdom into your life. You'll not be able to use them to help yourself.

Consciousness is something we all feel we have. But we often demonstrate that we don't have any idea what consciousness really is or how to open ourselves to divine love. Once we can open ourselves to God's love, we find that the answers come to us through God's Voice, the Holy Spirit, which we know as the ECK.

And how does God speak to us? God speaks through dreams, intuition, and sometimes the voices of other people who have more experience than we do. But unless we have opened our heart through singing HU, we won't have the discrimination to know wisdom when we hear it.

Scorched Irons

Ducks do strange things, but I sometimes think they're just following our lead. When we checked into the hotel, we requested an iron. Each iron we got was scorched and had gooey stuff on the bottom. If you heat up the iron and try to use it for its intended purpose, the stuff can stick and mess up your clothing.

The housekeeping staff went into a state of total amazement. They said, "Oh, my goodness! Look, there's gum on the bottom of this iron. We've never seen that before!"

One of the people in our party asked for an ironing board, but the one that was brought only had three of its four legs. Housekeeping was amazed at that too.

What was interesting about the irons was that they came to us scorched. We didn't scorch them, they came to us that way.

People usually don't recognize that everyone who comes into ECKANKAR brings along a scorched iron. They complain that it's scorched, but they don't realize it's their own iron.

I tell them, "You came to ECK with your own set of karmic problems. Now that they are coming back at you, you can't blame them on someone else." They scorched the iron themselves over a period of time, and now it's going to take a while to get it clean.

But people always want shortcuts. They don't want to accept that the iron was scorched by the heat of their own karma. Those of us who have had our eyes opened a little bit through the hard experience of life recognize and know this.

Next Step

I give these talks with the intention of eventually seeing them in book form. At this seminar we are releasing *The Book of ECK Parables,* Volume 3, which is compiled from stories I share in my talks. Though I hope the talks are enjoyable, with good editing they can also be turned into readable spiritual wisdom. Perhaps the stories will help you find the wisdom to go another step in ECK. And if you are going to tell others about ECK, the Holy Spirit, and God's love, you will have a book to offer them as a next step.

ECK Summer Festival, Anaheim, California,
Saturday, June 22, 1991

Yaubl Sacabi explained to her, "This is where the time of the universe is kept."

14

The Drumbeat of Time

In a restaurant last night I happened to spot a dessert display that featured small, overpriced slices of apple pie. I was so hungry that I had one anyway, and I can feel it this morning.

Using Discrimination with Foods

After a talk in which I mentioned foods I had found to be harmful to my system, somebody asked me, "What kinds of foods *can* we eat?" I was quite surprised at the question.

Basically, you can eat anything you want. Here's the point I was trying to make in my talk: If you don't feel as well as you should, then try to figure out what's causing the problem. Often you can trace it back to one of the foods in your diet.

Saturated Fats

Personal observation and study have convinced me that saturated fats really do cause many problems that we rarely attribute to our diet.

A flight attendant recently handed me one of those half-ounce packets of peanuts. Reading the printed matter on the packet, I found that the manufacturer had made a mistake and listed the nutritional information in a little box on the back. That half-ounce serving of peanuts contained seven grams of fat.

The American Heart Association recommends that a healthy diet would limit total calories from fat to 30 percent per day. That packet of peanuts would put you well on the way toward your total fat intake for the day.

Dr. Ornish, whose articles I have seen in several magazines over a period of time, has even stricter limits for total dietary fat. In his treatment of heart disease, he has found that a fair amount of healing occurs in patients who reduce their daily fat intake to only 10 percent of total calories per day. That little package of peanuts would account for a large part of their daily limit.

If you are determined to take in a lot of saturated fats, muffins and pies are excellent sources. Even that sliver of pie that I ate last night was loaded with it.

Benefits of Low-Fat Diet

It's very instructive to read the labels on foods in the grocery store. The fat and salt levels in foods such as potato chips and pretzels will give you a feel for what is considered a lot. I used to eat large amounts of potato chips back when I thought it was a perfectly healthy food. Maybe it is, but I'm not sure for whom.

I don't know if you'd call it frightening or convenient that there are fast-food restaurants everywhere now. Even if you stop eating their hamburgers and stick to chicken and fish, there's no real health gain if the food is deep-fried. Some fast-food restaurants have foods that are lower in fat; you just have to be selective.

Though I'm not a health practitioner, my personal study leads me to believe that a high-fat diet also diminishes our immune system somewhat.

I have also noticed that when I cut down on fat my voice is clearer. I can breathe better.

Saturated fats can cause problems for some people, especially as we get older. Most of our eating habits were established when we were young and active—when we could handle the fat. But as we age and become somewhat less active, our body becomes less able to burn off the fat. Sticking to the diet of our youth leaves us with a human machine that isn't as efficient as it once was, yet we're giving it the same fuel.

I don't always choose to eat a low-fat diet, though. As you get more gray hair, you convince yourself that there has to be a place in life for an ice-cream cone at least once a month. Or once a week.

Strengths and Weaknesses

Too much exposure to the sun can have an aging effect on the skin. We do need some sunlight, of course, but overdoing it can be harmful to people with lighter skin. Those with darker-colored skin, in Africa and other places where the climate is hot and sunny, have adapted over time; many of them find their skin can safely absorb more light.

People of every race have strengths and weaknesses. The challenge for each of us is to learn what they are so that we can make our life more enjoyable as we find our way back to God. Because where do we start to find our way back to God? Right here on earth.

Water

Medical professionals recommend that we drink six to eight glasses of water a day to aid in regular cleansing of the body. As soon as I get up in the morning, I force myself to drink two glasses of distilled water. I lost faith in spring water and tap water, but even they are better than not enough water.

As we age, the thirst response — the thing that tells us we're thirsty — begins not to work as well as when we were young. Not drinking enough water to flush out the impurities can lead to problems such as kidney stones, constipation, and aging of the skin.

Those of you who are into nutrition know that it's also a good idea to take a vitamin and mineral supplement. If we take these initiatives for our health, we can shortcut a lot of the problems that take up our time as we try to reach the higher states of spiritual realization.

Dairy Products

I grew up on a farm, and I like dairy products. But now they cause me problems. Every time I eat them, my sinuses close up tight. It feels like someone fed me a bale of cotton.

After I eat ice cream, even a small amount, my lower back also feels stiff and uncomfortable. It's as though my spine were out of place. It starts that evening and lasts through the next morning. Cutting back on the dairy products has helped this. Those of you who have lower-back problems might also want to cut back, just as a test. It's worth a try.

A Cleansed Vehicle

Last night I mentioned the scorched irons and the wobbly, three-legged ironing board that were sent by the hotel. The fact that the irons came to us scorched is an interesting parallel to the way people come to the path of ECK. They're scorched.

Before the iron can do the work for which it was intended, it has to go through a scrubbing process. It has to get rid of the gook and residue that has accumulated over time. Only then can this cleansed vehicle, used for its intended purpose, make the cloth of the spiritual body look smooth and beautiful.

A scorched iron can burn holes in the fabric. In other words, if you use an iron that has problems you only cause more problems. This is what happens when people try to fix themselves spiritually or solve an outer situation through their own means instead of relying on the Mahanta to set things straight. They find that their solutions actually burn more holes in more clothes.

The ironing board with only three legs was another example of how people come to the Living ECK Master. Like the wobbly ironing board, they are too out of balance to fulfill their function.

It's as if all the irons and ironing boards, in some way defective, come to the Master and say, "Fix me so that I can do a good job." But when you try to fix them, they complain.

Finding Your Way to Share ECK

This Year of the Vahana marks the beginning of our decade of missionary effort in ECK. To do my part, I gave an interview to two writers yesterday. They'll put together one or more articles, submit them to certain magazines, and see if they can generate interest in the teachings of ECK.

I've also gone on-line for ECK using my computer. About three years ago I subscribed to a computer information service, figuring there had to be a way to use it to tell people about ECK. I finally found a way.

There's a religion and ethics section in the information service that includes a bulletin board where you can submit a topic. I prepared a short paragraph, and just to get under people's skin and make them think, I gave it the title, "A God in Our Own Image?"

Not everyone will be interested in sharing the message of ECK through the computer network. There's quite a learning curve. Furthermore, there are so many other ways to participate in this missionary effort for ECK.

Those of you who have been helped in any way by your association with the Light and Sound of God can't help but want to give others the same opportunity. You won't be able to keep yourself from telling others.

On the other hand, if you are not aware of the help that comes to you from the Mahanta and the ECK, you're going to wonder what's the purpose of the ECK missionary program. You won't have anything to say or give to others, anyway.

A God in Our Own Image?

There was an article in the May 1991 *Reader's Digest,* "Religion: The Great Untold Story." The author begins by creating a scenario in which a fictitious pitcher, who has just tossed a no-hitter, is asked by a reporter: "To what do you credit your success?" "God," says the pitcher.

The article goes on to other things and gets better from there. But it left me with this question: Is God really into sports? If two high-school teams go to the state finals and each prays for victory, whom does God help? Does He have a team preference?

And after the big game, how often do you hear a coach say, "God helped us win"? Our hero is more likely to puff on and on about his clever game plan.

Nor do you ever hear a coach blame God for a loss. Our God is a very handy God; in fact, if you accept some people's descriptions of God's will, He is just like us. Thus the title of my computer communication, "A God in Our Own Image?"

Sharing Experiences with HU

This is the message I put on the computer bulletin board: "Want to look for the real God within you? Try this little song from an old, sacred name for God, HU. Sing it as H-U-U (like the word *hue*) in one long sound, in one long breath. Repeat it aloud or silently for five minutes when you're alone. See what happens. Give it a few days or a week. More later."

A few of the comments I got back were almost profane. One was from a person who had been in Vietnam and evidently returned with strong psychological problems.

A welcome response turned out to be from a good friend of ours who used the screen name of "Larro." His message read: "I've had pretty good luck with HU. I'm curious about your experiences."

These messages come via a feature called E-mail, which stands for electronic mail. E-mail gives subscribers sort of a private mailbox in the post office section of the computer system. These communication networks have everything you'd find out here—bulletin boards, a post office, meeting rooms—except that it's all on the screen.

195

I downloaded the message from Larro and showed it to my wife. "Where's it from?" she asked.

"Brooklyn, New York."

"I bet that's Larry," my wife said, referring to a Higher Initiate in ECK. She was right.

Vahana Aid

Larry and I began to talk with each other on-line. He supported me by leaving a message with his point of view on the subject of "A God in Our Own Image?"

In the meantime, he also put his own ECK message on the bulletin board. He began a discussion based on "The Mirror of God," a chapter from *Stranger by the River.* I was pleased to see that a few ECKists came on-line to support him, with comments such as, "I tried it. It works!" It appears that computers will prove to be a fantastic vehicle for the ECK.

A RESA up in the Northwest Territories in Canada, where they have miles and miles of empty space and few people, told me that some of the ECKists there now use computers and E-mail too. Whereas it used to take a few days to get responses by regular mail, he now sends a note by computer and someone gets back to him the very same day.

In a short time, more and more of our communication is going to be done through E-mail. The computer technology of today will be a real aid in the ECK Vahana program.

To those of you who support the message of ECK on the computer network or in any other way, thank you very much. Your efforts are helping us build a spiritual community in many different ways, on many different levels.

The Useless Son

Study of the ECK discourses can bring us insight into who and what we were in a previous life. This can lead to a better understanding of who we are today and why certain things are happening to us.

An ECKist had an experience many years before she ever heard of the ECK teachings. As a child of seven, she had felt useless, unloved, unwanted. Then one night in her dreams the ECK Master Yaubl Sacabi came to her.

She found herself standing in a desert with him, near a small encampment. A dust storm blew up, and people ran for shelter. Nearby she saw a little man trying to get some camels to move, but they wouldn't budge. First he cursed the camels, and when that didn't work, he began to curse his son.

"Where's that useless son, Yaubl?" he shouted. "I hoped he would take over the family business and make something of himself. But he's always off with his head in the clouds."

The seven-year-old girl stood and listened to Yaubl Sacabi's father call him useless. Yaubl then turned to her and said, "Everything I have I will always give to anyone else who needs it." It wasn't until years later, when she read similar words in *The Shariyat-Ki-Sugmad,* that she made the connection and understood what he was saying.

Yaubl spoke to her many times after that in her dreams during her childhood, always above the angry scolding of his father. It was in this setting that he explained the spiritual wisdom of ECK to this little girl who also felt useless and unwanted. On the inner planes, the ECK Masters come to each individual in a way they can relate to at that moment, regardless of age.

197

Drumbeat of Time

The girl grew up, became a member of ECKANKAR, and began to study the *ECK Dream Discourses*. Shortly after she tried the spiritual exercise in the first discourse, she started to hear a drumbeat, not only during contemplation but in her outer life too. She also heard an unusual kind of flute music.

The flute music and the drumbeat were actually forms of the Sound of God. The Sound is one of the ways that the Holy Spirit or the ECK speaks to people.

About this time, someone gave her son an audiocassette of synthesized music. The first time she sat down to listen to it, she heard a flute playing in a certain way, combined with ocean sounds. It was very much like the melody she had heard inwardly during contemplation after she began *The ECK Dream Discourses*.

That song ended and another began, this one with a familiar drumbeat. She closed her eyes to listen more closely. Soon the drumbeat carried over into a contemplative state, where again she met with Yaubl Sacabi.

This time he took her out into space. Nothing was visible in the absolute empty space except for a ledge. Then she saw tall, thin, pale men, walking back and forth along a pathway on this ledge. She knew they were masters.

Suspended in space, where you'd have to fly to get there, was something that looked like a huge sundial with a series of big cogwheels and gears. Occasionally one of the masters had to go out there to make an adjustment. He would simply head in the direction of this assembly of machines, and a rock would appear under his feet for him to walk on. The rock stayed under his feet long enough for him to walk out there, make the necessary adjustments to the time gears, then return to the ledge.

This ECKist was getting ready for her Second Initiation in a couple of months. Years ago, when I was about to receive the Second Initiation, I went to this very same place.

Yaubl Sacabi explained to her, "This is where the time of the universe is kept."

She heard a steady drumbeat, much like the drumbeat on her son's audiocassette, coming from the clock mechanisms. "It sounds like the drumbeat on a Roman galley," she said.

Immediately she found herself on one of those Roman ships. There was a tall, strong man with reddish hair, reddish beard, and sunken eyes. First she saw him from the outside, but an instant later she found herself inside this man, experiencing everything that was going on from his viewpoint. He was an oarsman. She was seeing herself in a past life.

Lessons from a Past Life

The first thing that struck her was the smell. It was musty, as it would be from the bodies of the other oarsmen below deck with her, rowing and rowing.

The only light below deck came through the holes where the oars poked out. Through those same oar holes also came frigid ocean spray. It was a cold, dark, miserable existence.

There was no hope of life in the sunken eyes of the man she had been. He was so thirsty. But rather than ask the cruel overseer for a drink of water, he would wait until the next one came on duty.

Down the walkway came the cruel overseer. The very sight of him inspired overwhelming hate and anger. Though he looked different, she knew immediately that this man was her husband in this lifetime.

A few days later her husband noticed her reading an ECK discourse. Her husband, who is not a member of ECK, asked her, "Well, what are they trying to teach you now?"

"They're trying to teach me how not to hate you," she'd answered. And she understood how true this was.

People rarely understand why they are drawn to certain relationships. As a couple they get along all right. He doesn't abuse her; he doesn't act like an overseer. But between them there is an opposition, a tension. It was brought here from the past.

What she didn't see, of course, were the lives in which she was in the role of the overseer and he was the oarsman. Life gives you an opportunity to scorch your iron from both ends.

More to ECK than Experiences

The woman who met Yaubl Sacabi and went into the past had many of these experiences long before she came to ECK. As a child, she had no idea what they meant. The first time she heard the Sound of God, she feared she was losing her mind.

Some of the people in her Satsang class have said, "I'd do anything to have your experiences."

"Experiences are not why I stay in ECK," she tells them. "I stay because of the understanding I'm gaining through the ECK teachings of what those experiences mean."

Spiritual Overview

These are momentous times in ECKANKAR, though many people may not realize it yet. We have recently released a book, *The Temple of ECK,* that chronicles the construction and dedication of the Temple of ECK. You might call it a historical keepsake. As we live our life and work through so many of our own problems, we often don't get the spiritual overview of what is taking place.

The Temple doesn't mean that our existence here as a spiritual path is assured. It's not. We're going to have to fight every inch of the way. But some of you have seen the vision of ECKANKAR as a world teaching—truly a world teaching. Today we are a small group, but we have begun the missionary effort to find those who have already been touched by the Light and Sound of God.

There are many more people in the world today who have already made some contact with the Light and Sound of God. Now we're simply going to find them.

You're going to be finding old friends; we've all been together before. And as we come together now and in the future, we will form the spiritual community of ECK.

Seminar Gifts

Some of you are wondering how you're going to absorb everything you have been given this weekend. Believe me, anything you have noticed out here is only one-tenth of what has occurred. At least nine-tenths of everything that has changed in you spiritually has happened on the inner planes. But once you go home, you'll have time to digest what you have seen, felt, and experienced here.

In the weeks to come, suddenly some little tidbit you heard here at the seminar will come to mind, perhaps when you have a problem with your car or some other minor crisis. As you work to resolve the problem, you'll begin to understand how this particular incident came about to help make you a stronger spiritual being, a stronger spiritual you.

I would like to wish all of you a safe journey home—
to your home here and also to that home in the Far
Country in the other worlds, to the Ocean of Love and
Mercy. May the blessings be.

ECK Summer Festival, Anaheim, California,
Sunday, June 23, 1991

Like the birds, we don't always stop to think that maybe life or God has arranged the incident for our spiritual unfoldment and for the good of everybody else.

15

A Long Journey of Many Seasons
Part 1

An ECK initiate, who is retired, likes to go to ECK seminars whenever she can. She wanted to attend the seminar here in The Hague but didn't think she would have enough money.

"How did you get here?" I asked when I saw her.

"I bought a lottery ticket," she confided. "I won just enough to pay my way here."

An Agreement with the ECK

She had set it in her mind that she wanted to take this trip, played the lottery in her home country, and won just the amount that she needed.

"Congratulations," I said.

"This is the third time," she admitted.

I wanted to get this straight. I said, "Did you win a little bit the first time, which wasn't quite enough, then a little bit more the second time and it still wasn't enough, so you played a third time?"

"Oh, no," she said. "Three times, three seminars." Then she added, "Now I'm thinking of attending the Worldwide Seminar in Minneapolis this October."

"Do the lottery stakes run that high?" I asked.

"I don't really know," she said, "but it doesn't hurt to try."

If there is something you want in life, do everything within your power to bring it about. When you haven't the power to do any more, Divine Spirit will help you in some way.

This doesn't mean that just because you decide to go to a certain seminar, the heavens will open up and pour wheelbarrows of money into your yard. It works for this woman because it's her way; it's her agreement with the ECK.

It's not my way, I can assure you. I never did very well at those things. The first time I'd play one of the games, I would win; after that, I'd pay and pay and pay, believing that somehow my luck would change to good again. But over the years I've learned that I have to earn it as I go.

Weathering Change

The birds back home in Minnesota used to hang around in our front yard to be near the feeder, but their droppings were just not the right kind of fertilizer for our trees. When the trees began dying, I had to move the feeder to the backyard.

"I think they're smart enough to find the food," I told my wife. "They fly high enough to see the feeder on top of the pole. If I move it just a few yards around to the back, they should have no problem."

The sparrows found it soon enough, but not without comment. You never saw such a commotion. As they flew around to the back, they spouted things like, "Cheep-cheep-cheep."

206

"Cheap?" I said. "Cheap? You birds don't know the price of seed!" But sparrows don't take offense at anything.

Then there were the other birds. They went to the place in the front yard were the feeder had been, and when they couldn't find it, they complained loudly, "It should be here, it should be here, it should be here."

I said from the backyard, "Too bad but it's here, too bad but it's here, too bad but it's here." They were very upset.

Birds are much the same as people, or maybe I should say we are much the same as birds. If one little thing in our life changes, something we hadn't planned on, we fly around squawking, "Cheap, cheap, cheap," as in "cheap trick, cheap trick, cheap trick."

Like the birds, we don't always stop to think that maybe life or God has arranged the incident for our spiritual unfoldment and for the good of everybody else. In this case, the message to the birds was, "If you keep feeding in the front yard, you'll kill all the trees. If we move the feeder to the backyard, you'll still be able to eat. And the trees can live too. We're making this change for the good of everybody."

We too may not understand what's going on when the powers of life move in and rearrange our life: we lose a job, we lose a spouse, or sometimes we put a dent in a brand-new car.

An ECKist told me a very sad story along this line. The day she brought her brand-new car home, she triggered the automatic garage-door opener, then sped into the garage before the door had a chance to open all the way. The entire top of the car was dented. I sat there and almost cried. That's pain, all right.

The Rabbit and the Flowers

Last year I got a little upset with the rabbit that comes to our house. I had planted flowers in the front yard. It made me very proud when the neighbors came by and said, "What pretty flowers you have."

I like to make things beautiful. As long as we are here on earth, I feel that we should leave it just a little bit better than we found it.

The first year I planted flowers, I spent too much time on the kinds that needed grooming every few minutes. It took me a lot of time each day to groom the geraniums. You don't have to, but they look better if you do.

Last year I planted marigolds. You cannot destroy a marigold. You put them in the ground, and that's pretty much it.

The rabbit was quite tame by then. Just before the sun went down, he would come to the yard to wait for feeding time. But one night I went outside to find him eating the marigolds. He must have been too hungry to wait for the seed.

When I scolded him, he looked at me in surprise and shock. He couldn't figure out why this nice man who had provided him with these flowers was suddenly behaving this way. Puzzled, he scampered off to hide.

Later I told my wife, "I feel really bad about the rabbit, but the flowers have rights too." After that, the rabbit stayed way back, and this year my flowers did OK—for a while.

Then I noticed that the marigolds hadn't bloomed. I fertilized them, but they still didn't bloom.

"I think the rabbit's eating the flowers again," I complained to my wife.

"He wouldn't eat the flowers," she said. She always defends the rabbit.

"Just wait till I catch him."

One day I looked out the window, and there he was in the backyard, eating the buds off the marigolds. I guess he likes the buds because they're very tender. I couldn't believe my eyes when he went up to a big, full, yellow flower and opened his mouth. "He wouldn't dare," I said, then watched as he took a big chomp out of it, leaving only half a flower.

I called to my wife, "The rabbit did it again!"

"No! He didn't!" she said.

"If you hurry, you'll see where the yellow went." But by the time she got to the window, the rest of the flower had disappeared into his mouth.

A Long Journey of Many Seasons

I have since come to an agreement with nature. I figure if I want to plant flowers, that's my business; if the rabbit wants to eat them, that's his business. We get along fine now. I smile at him, he looks back at me, and that's how we pass our time. We both love flowers.

This is the long journey of many seasons. We have many experiences as we go through life, and many of them aren't as simple as trying to debate with the birds or rabbits: Should the feeder be moved? Should you eat the flowers? Sometimes we get into the bigger problems of life that make us wonder, What is this all about?

Spiritual Riches

Recently I said to my wife, "Wouldn't it be a shame if people thought the only reason they came into this life was

209

to learn how to invest their money better? What an empty, useless existence."

There's nothing wrong with money; there certainly is nothing wrong with investing it. It's perfectly all right to have the good things in life. But there has to be something more. If there isn't, no matter how much material wealth one has, that individual is very poor indeed.

Spiritual riches have very little, if anything, to do with how much money you have in the bank. You may have a lot or you may have none. If you have none but are happy to wake up in the morning to face the day and meet your responsibilities, then you are a fortunate person. You are one of the rich ones. In the important ways, you are richer than anyone who has expensive cars, boats, and homes.

The teachings of ECK help people find a way to make sense out of this life. We all want to understand why we're who we are, why we have what we have. But even more, we want to know why we don't have what we think we should have.

Broader Perspective

What brought us to where we are today? The answer is very simple: We have put ourselves exactly where we belong.

Someone who has no understanding of karma and reincarnation will say, "That's wrong. I was born into my family. I had no say in how much or how little wealth we had, the state of my health in my life, or how the people in my family treated me. God put me here, but I don't know why."

But once you add the equation of karma and reincarnation, as many of the eastern religions have done, your perspective on life is broadened. All of a sudden many things that never used to make any sense begin to reveal a pattern.

Before the individual can find truth, he must be introduced to the basic teachings of karma and reincarnation. You and I are Soul, you and I have walked this earth many times in the past.

Where Will You Serve God?

When they first come on the path of ECK, many people hope that they will never have to walk this earth again.

The feeling at first is almost a selfish one. "I'm tired of this place of pain and suffering," they say. "If there is a teaching that will show me the way out of here, so that I need never return again, then I will listen to what that path has to say."

But at some point in your spiritual unfoldment, you'll become so filled with the love of God that there will be no room left inside you for selfish thoughts. It won't matter to you whether you come back here in another life to serve as a Co-worker with God or go on to one of the many heavens on the other planes.

When you can come to the spiritual agreement within yourself that it doesn't matter where you serve God, then you will have reached the highest degree of truth and wisdom that is available anywhere.

We are not trying to find truth in the form of so many words or to find wisdom as some undefined quality. What we are trying to do is to become the path of truth ourselves, so that wherever we are, we recognize the presence of God; wherever we walk, we know we walk on holy ground. This is what we are trying to achieve on the path of ECK.

Malaria Pills

We're going to Africa for the ECK seminar in Nigeria next weekend. That requires certain shots and pills. The malaria pills have to be taken a week before you get there, the day you get there, then once a week for the next four weeks.

After the talk last night, my wife and I went to a restaurant with a few friends who will be traveling to Africa with us. One of them happened to mention that he was scheduled to begin his pills on Sunday. I turned to another person. "By the way, did you take your malaria pills?"

"I forgot," he said.

"Don't worry," I said. "We'll remind you before you get back to your room." But by the time we finished the meal, we had all forgotten about it.

I awoke abruptly in the middle of the night. "We forgot to tell him to take his malaria pill," I told my wife. We had just about settled back to sleep when I remembered something else. "But he has to take it with food."

"We'll remind him in the morning," she said sleepily. "One day won't hurt anything." This was somewhere between two and five o'clock in the morning.

When we saw him at breakfast, he said, "I woke up at five o'clock this morning and heard you say very clearly, 'You have to take your malaria pill.' So I got up, took the pill, crawled back in bed, and pulled the covers over me. Just as I was about to go back to sleep, I heard you say, 'But you have to take it with food.'

"So I pulled back the covers again, got up, and found some cookies. After I ate them and drank some water, I got back in bed and lay there thinking, I hope I can get some sleep now. I hope I did everything right this time."

The person who's on the Sunday schedule then piped in, "I woke up in the middle of the night too. I don't know why, but it just seemed like it was time to get up and take my malaria pill. I also remembered that I had to take food with it."

Someone else joked, "Wouldn't it be funny if you told this story at the seminar and all the people in the audience who are going to Africa stood up and said, 'So that's why I got up in the middle of the night and took my pill.'"

Ray's Long Journey

On the plane from the U.S. my wife took the aisle seat and I was in the center. Finally the person who had the window seat arrived—a tall gentleman who resembled the comedian Jerry Lewis. "It's always the latecomer who sits by the window," he said. Though grumping and grousing even as he got seated, he was not at all offensive.

"No problem," we said. "We didn't even buckle up because we knew you would be coming."

"My name's Ray," the man said as he squeezed his large frame into the seat and struggled to fold his long legs into the cramped space in front of him.

"I'm Harold, and this is my wife, Joan," I said.

"Pleased to meet you." Ray was a tough-talking guy but we found him very amiable. He's the kind of person you just like, no matter what he says.

"They got us traveling back here like cattle," he groused. "If we wanted to pay more than this flight is worth, we could sit up there in first class. But I'm not going to pay that kind of money. And anyway," he added, "I got the reading material to go with this class." He looked kind of embarrassed as he showed me his copy of the *National Enquirer.*

Every year the airplane seats seem to get narrower and the knee space shorter. When an empty water container fell off the table between my wife and me, I didn't have enough room to bend down to pick it up. "Kick it back to the kids," my grumpy seat companion suggested.

There were two children seated behind us. Something seems to compel children on an airplane to kick the seat in front of them. Maybe it's part of their genetic code. In the past I've been seated with a child behind me and another in front. The one in front kept rocking his seat back and forth while the one behind me was kicking the back of my seat.

Ray's seat had just been kicked from behind and he was quite upset. "In another minute, I'm going back there to straighten this out," he threatened. He was such a rough character that I decided I'd better share some airplane etiquette with him to keep him from being arrested.

I said, "When a child does that, I usually turn around and talk with the parent. I say, 'Listen, I need to get some rest. Would you please ask your child to stop kicking the back of my seat?'"

Ray wasn't too impressed. "We'll just wait and see how it goes," he said.

As Ray began to tell us about himself, I saw that his life truly had been a long journey of many seasons. He had seen many hard things. "I was born on Saturday, December 13," he said. "Missed Friday the thirteenth by only one day. And from that point on, my life went downhill."

Though likable, Ray had very strong, definite opinions and didn't hesitate to state them. It's best to let a person like that have his opinions—especially if you're smaller.

"Yeah," he went on, "my wife left me, I got a divorce, and I said, 'Well, I'm not going to cry about that.' I always wanted a Corvette—a fancy sports car, you know—so I decided to get one."

Ray ordered the car and waited for his registration and other paperwork to arrive in the mail. One day he received a strange green envelope. He quickly tore it open, expecting some kind of notification about delivery of his car. What he found instead was a letter informing him: "You have been inducted into the United States Army." This was on April Fool's Day, by the way.

"I couldn't believe my eyes," Ray said. He'd had a deferment because of his marital status and hadn't yet notified anyone of the change. "I think my wife told the army about the divorce."

So he got drafted and was sent to army boot camp for very rigorous training. When he graduated, an officer called him in and said, "You're in big trouble."

"What for?" Ray asked.

"You got a traffic ticket when you were fifteen. You neglected to put it on the forms when you enlisted in the army."

"Enlisted? You drafted me!" Ray said. "If I've done something that wrong, by all means, throw me out of here and let me go home."

They put him on a plane to Vietnam. This was in 1965, about the time the war had just begun to heat up. One of the first American soldiers over there, Ray had to help set up the army bases. He also spent time in combat. *Stars and Stripes*, the military newspaper, wrote an article about his heroic actions and how he had cleverly repaired his machine gun with a ballpoint pen.

"The firing pin on my machine gun had gotten stuck," Ray recalled. "I was in the thickest part of the jungle and couldn't see much, but I managed to take the weapon apart."

The only soldier in that position, Ray knew the enemy troops were edging closer. He repaired his weapon and did what he had to do to defend his life.

The soldiers who came in later to rescue him said, "You know, Ray, you made a mess back there. Do you want to go see?"

"I've seen enough," he told them. "I don't want to see any more." He had been forced to fight for his life, and the aftermath was very difficult for him.

Just before Ray was to be sent home, he was given the assignment of cook. He could have taken it easy for the rest of his tour. Instead, he asked to be transferred back to the field where, in one way or another, he found ways to get steaks for the new troops who were just coming in. "I never got food like that," he said. "I wanted good stuff for the guys who came after me."

A friend who flew a helicopter helped him transport the steaks to his unit. He was then able to serve excellent meals to the troops who were lucky enough to have him as their cook.

When Ray returned to the States, he picked up his Corvette, moved into a trailer, and began to put his life back together. Though he still conducted trainings for the military, he was greatly relieved to be back home.

One day he was outside by his trailer, washing his car. Suddenly he heard the sound of gunshots. He looked up to see a man at one end of his trailer shooting at another guy who was crouched at the other end. Ray was right in the middle of a gunfight. The man closest to him issued a warning: "If you don't want to get hurt, you'd better move out of the way."

Ray just shook his head. "I couldn't believe this was happening right in my own trailer court. But like I said, ever since the day I was born—December 13—my life has gone downhill."

This is the kind of life some people go through—and worse.

Ray had become a fireman, and he was retiring on his next birthday. He pointed out that, "It falls on Friday the thirteenth this year. I don't know what to expect."

Soul's Awareness

Ray was an interesting person. He went through life making his own breaks wherever he could. "This is the first time I've left the States since Vietnam," he said. Someone had invited him to travel around England for two weeks. "People are always inviting me to go someplace with them, because wherever I go, things happen."

"I can believe that," I said.

Ray is a person on a long journey of many seasons, but he has no idea what it's about or why he gets these experiences. It is Soul going through one life, which follows many previous lifetimes.

Soul eventually reaches a point where It becomes aware that It has heard the Sound and seen the Light of God. In ECK we recognize that the Sound and Light, the two aspects of the Holy Spirit, are real; they are actual things.

Developing Your Inner Hearing

Those who have developed the inner hearing can hear this Sound of God in one or more of its many forms. Sometimes it sounds just like a flute, an orchestra, or even a bird singing. Other times it is heard as a thunderstorm when there is no storm outside, or as a drum roll when there's no one around playing drums.

These are some of the Sounds of God which uplift you spiritually. To hear them means that you have come to a certain high point in life where you are ready to step onto the path of ECK.

This is why it is so important for us in ECK to let others know about the Light and Sound of God. Many people today, knowing nothing about ECK, have heard one of these Sounds of God but have no idea what it means.

Golden Opportunity

Others have seen one of the many different manifestations of the Light of God, or they may have seen people appear as beings of light. Again, they have no idea what this image of light means to them spiritually.

You have to tell them; you have to bring the message of the Light and Sound of God to people who are waiting for the same opportunity that you have.

And what is this opportunity? It's to be filled with the love of God. Because without the love of God, this life has no meaning. You might as well go out and try to get the best rate of interest on your money. That is the most this life will ever bring you, unless you have the true knowledge of God.

ECK European Seminar, The Hague, The Netherlands,
Saturday, July 20, 1991

The music of God is sometimes heard as a flute, string instruments, a bird, thunder, the roll of drums, and many other sounds. Mozart is one example of a man who heard the Sound of God.

16

A Long Journey of Many Seasons
Part 2

Last evening I told how I had awoken in the middle of the night and mentioned to my wife that we had forgotten to remind one of the ECKists to take his malaria pill. He'll be traveling to Africa for the ECK seminar next weekend, and the pills have to be started a week ahead of time.

Since there was nothing we could do about it right then, we went back to sleep. The next morning he told us that he had woken up at 5:00 a.m. and clearly heard me tell him to take his malaria pill.

We all thought it would be pretty funny if I told this story on stage and everyone who was going to Africa stood up and said, "So that's why I woke up and took my malaria pill."

Inner Communication

As soon as I left the stage I ran into another person who's going to the African seminar. He said, "When I woke up this morning, the first thing that popped into my mind was malaria pills. I asked my wife, 'When do we have to start taking our malaria pills?' She said, 'Oops, two days ago.' " Fortunately, they got the message in time.

There is an inner communication in ECK. And it works. Many people don't understand what this means, and there simply is no way to explain it to anyone who hasn't had the experience.

It doesn't necessarily come as a voice speaking to you. Sometimes it's a simple knowing—suddenly you just know something very strongly, and you act on it. The best way you can explain why you did what you did is to say, "I had a strong feeling to do it."

This is the intuition at work. This is yourself as a spiritual being responding to the Mahanta, the spiritual state of consciousness that tries to help you make your life better.

Making the Best of Your Life

Last night I talked about Ray, the man who sat next to me on the flight to Europe. Born on Saturday, December 13, he missed Friday the thirteenth by one day. From that day on, he said, everything had gone downhill.

Ray told me one story after another about the bad luck he had experienced throughout his life. "Actually," he said, "I did have some good luck, but I used up most of it in Vietnam."

What I found interesting was that Ray didn't give up and surrender to the supposed negative forces in his life. After his discharge from the army, he took a job with the fire department, where he has worked for many years. He plans to retire on his birthday in December.

In the meantime, he said, he has taken part-time jobs to develop other skills so that he can continue to work after his retirement. At that point, he'll be able to choose his own hours and play golf the rest of the time.

One of his part-time jobs is for a small car-rental

agency with a service counter at the airport. The only way they can compete with the bigger rental agencies, Ray said, is to provide better, more personalized service. When a customer calls to reserve a vehicle, a company representative picks him up at the airport and takes him right to the car. Ray's job is to make the whole transaction as smooth as possible for the customer.

One of the friends he made was a top executive in the travel business. Ray was so accommodating that this man and his wife began to ask for him whenever they needed a rental car.

Despite all his hard luck, Ray always did the best he could, never settling for less. Although he didn't have a high-level job in the car-rental agency, the travel executive came to respect him for his skills. In time they developed a friendship.

One day the executive called him and said, "My son is moving up north. Could you put him up in your cottage for a while?" Ray had a cottage in the northern part of the United States, where he happened to be at the time, and a home down south.

"Sure," Ray said. "I'll leave the key under the mat." The young man found a job, moved his family to the area, and eventually moved out of the cottage. Soon after that, Ray got a phone call from the executive. "Any time you need to travel somewhere, let me know," the man said. "I can be of help to you."

One of Ray's out-of-state relatives got sick and had to have an operation. Ray called the travel executive for help in making flight arrangements. "Sure, I can get you a seat," his friend said. He got Ray a very good seat for about half price, much less than it would have cost through a travel agency.

Even when Ray had to change the reservations three times because the relative's surgery kept being rescheduled, the executive said, "No problem. Just call me any time." Now whenever Ray wants to take a trip, he just calls up his friend. Arrangements are made immediately, and the ticket arrives in the mail within a day or two.

Looking for the Best in Others

Because Ray always did his best, he attracted like-minded people. Friendships are bound to develop as you come across those who share the same values that you do.

This is what the friendship among the Brothers of the Leaf—the Higher Initiates in ECK—should be based on. Often it is not. People do not always make an effort to look for the good in each other.

I learned the importance of this at a very young age. As a six-year-old child working on a threshing crew, I had a disappointing experience with three people I admired very much. One was a minister who gave up a baseball career to serve God. Another was the grade-school teacher whom I considered the wisest among men. The third was Gust, a mischievous old man with a kindly, compassionate spirit.

That one experience taught me that even though each man had his strong qualities, he also had his weaknesses. I then had to decide, Do I throw away my esteem for these three individuals just because they have human weaknesses? It was my first clue that no one is either completely good or completely bad.

There are many Higher Initiates who have this esteem for each other. I would hope that those who haven't already done so would try a little harder to look for the best in each other. Heaven knows there are enough weaknesses. But when you are working together, when you have a job to do, it is especially important to focus on the strengths that you share.

God's Music

Wolfgang Mozart was a musician whose broad achievements epitomize the spirit of doing the best that one is capable of doing. Perhaps the greatest composer to come out of the western world, the excellence of his music lives on even two hundred years after his death. Why? Because he heard the Sound Current of God.

This music of God is sometimes heard as a flute, string instruments, a bird, thunder, the roll of drums, and many other sounds. Because Mozart could hear this heavenly music more directly, he often wrote down his scores all the way through. Whereas Beethoven had to struggle, change, correct, and rewrite his compositions again and again, Mozart was usually able to get it right the first time.

When questioned about this ability, he said that he didn't hear the music in pieces or in sequence; he heard it all together at once. In other words, it didn't come to him a little bit at a time so he would have to piece it together. He said of this gift, "I can't tell you how wonderful it is."

People ask, "What do you mean by the music of God? What do you mean by the Sound of God?" Mozart is one example of a man who heard the Sound of God and tried to put It into a form that we could enjoy and appreciate, even today.

What makes great people great? In some way, they can see the Light of God or hear the Sound of God. To see the Light of God is a great accomplishment by itself; to hear the Sound of God is a greater accomplishment.

225

Mozart heard the Voice of God speaking in one of Its true ways—through this heavenly music. He also could copy down, note for note, whatever he heard.

Sin versus Karma

I won't say Mozart's music is quiet and peaceful, but then the music of God isn't always quiet and peaceful. Sometimes it's loud; it seems to tear. You might think that the music of God would always be beautiful and soft, but sometimes it has to tear.

Why? Because Soul has these impurities, these burdens of karma—burdens of sin, if you will—that It has been carrying for many lifetimes. But *sin* is a term that doesn't provide a full enough description.

The difference between sin and karma is this: Sin is the most shallow understanding of a symptom of something that is wrong in a person's spiritual character. The concept of sin doesn't encompass the depth and quality of the true error or mistake that a person has made sometime in the past.

Karma has the depth and dimension of centuries and lifetimes behind it. Sin basically has only a two-dimensional aspect. Original sin, for instance, is something you couldn't help, something that happened just because you were born.

So where does that leave you, as a creative child of God? Nowhere. You're stuck from the day you land in the mud of earth. That's not a very uplifting spiritual philosophy at all.

Those Who Hear the Music

We are looking for a way to hear the Sound of God, the music that Mozart heard. Once you hear It, you

226

become a lighter, happier person. Mozart was just that, as well as a little bit lewd and a lot of other things. But overall he was full of life, something that Beethoven was not. That's my feeling, and I may have to leave the stage quickly to avoid avid Beethoven fans.

Beethoven was one of the great composers. But he was almost a scholastic type of musician to whom the music of God came very laboriously.

Beethoven had to work through a physical body which wasn't attuned to the music out here. That made it practically impossible for him to put down in notes the music that he heard inwardly. He heard it with great difficulty. With his physical deafness, which began when he was twenty-eight, it's a wonder that he could write music at all.

Scale of Life

Whenever you see great men or women—people who have accomplished something useful or uplifting that thousands of others have not—look for some connection in their life with the Light or Sound of God. It's always there. On the other hand, as you look into the lives of history's great tyrants, you find no evidence of Light or Sound.

These are two extremes on the scale of life. Most of humanity is somewhere in between these extremes. Some are further up or even lower on the scale. There are the Mozarts and there are the Hitlers; that's just how it is in this world.

And as we criticize the Hitlers and praise the Mozarts, let's keep in mind that in each human being there is a little bit of Hitler, just as there is a great deal of Mozart. Remembering this will keep us humble.

For now, Mozart is the best example I can give of a person who heard the Sound of God. For those of you who would like to listen to some of his music, *Eine kleine Nachtmusik* and *The Magic Flute* are very pretty.

Singing to God

The best way to make contact with the Light and Sound of God is through the Spiritual Exercises of ECK. One of these is simply to sing HU, a name for God. This is your love song to God, to be sung in your own way, in your own unique style. If you feel uncomfortable with HU, then sing some other word or name for God that has a soft, poetic feel to it.

The English word *God,* with the hard G sound, doesn't come out very well as a chant. But HU, chanted as HU-U-U-U, has a very nice sound. Embodied in that one word are all the sounds of creation: the singing of birds, crickets, frogs and other sounds of nature, the symphonies, chamber music and operas of Mozart, the country-western music, and possibly even rock.

The inner communication works only because of the Sound of God. When God speaks from the Ocean of Love and Mercy, from the Heart of God, the Sound comes down through the worlds as a great wave. This is the Voice of God, sometimes referred to as the Audible Sound Current; in Christianity It is called the Holy Spirit. When the Mahanta, the Inner Master—who is the spiritual leader of ECK—speaks, it is upon this wave, the Sound Current that comes from the Ocean of Love and Mercy.

This Voice of God is no more a person than God is a person. Any confusion in understanding stems from the human consciousness trying to explain the infinite being in finite terms. Even today there are people who become very upset at the suggestion that God is not a person, that the Holy Spirit is not a person.

I am saying It is something other. The nearest you can come to hearing the Voice of God, and therefore following the will of God and finding the love of God, is through the Sound Current, the sound of HU.

I don't expect you to take it on my authority or on anybody else's, so I am giving you the song of HU. Sing the word HU. If you are ready, in a very short time— anywhere up to six months—you will have some definite recognition of a change for the better in your spiritual life. There will be some kind of communication from God, directly or indirectly, that will bring upliftment to your life that was never there before.

The HU Book

An ECK initiate is the grandmother of a six-year-old boy. Before their divorce, the boy's parents were both ECKists. The entire family knew and sang HU, and the boy often saw the Inner Master.

After the divorce, the mother married a man from another culture and another religion. The new stepfather not only tried to stop the child from singing HU, he sought to break all connection the boy had with the path of ECK.

But the boy knew the Sound of God, he had seen the Light of God in the form of the Blue Star and as a blue light, and he traveled on the inner planes with the Mahanta. The stepfather didn't know this, of course. His was a very rigid, intolerant religion that had no room for love; no room to love anybody whose beliefs were different from his.

I mention this as a reminder. We in ECK come from just about every religion on earth. We too have suffered intolerance as we tried to leave our old religion and come to ECK. If we remember this, and have any awareness of the true spirit of a spiritual path, we will always allow others the freedom of their own religion, even though it is not ECK.

The stepfather was not always kind to the boy, often treating him poorly. The grandmother was very concerned. "Is this karma between my grandson and his stepfather?" she asked.

It is karma, and what she can do is just love them both more. While the son works off some karmic debt that he has created with his stepfather in the past, he is also gaining strength.

Right after the marriage, the stepfather cleared all the ECK books and materials from the home. But each time the boy visited his grandmother, he would say, "Where's my HU book? Let's go look for my HU book." To humor him, the grandmother took him to several bookstores to look for this HU book, but they could never find it.

About a year later we published a book about the HU. The grandmother bought a copy, but on the day her daughter's family was to visit her home, she hid it in the bookcase behind some other books so as not to cause offense. The daughter no longer follows ECK.

But as soon as the family came in the door the grandson said, "Where's my HU book?" He then walked straight to the bookcase, removed the books in front, reached in, and pulled it out. "Here it is," he said. "Here's my HU book."

The child knew about the book because he had already seen it before we produced it. We produced it because it was a creation already on the inner planes, already manifested at a particular level of the Light and Sound of God.

230

The boy's connection with the Mahanta, the Living ECK Master is very strong. It is an inner communication built upon the Light and Sound of God.

Healing Your Heart

The Light and Sound of God is the heart of any true religion. Yet, strangely enough, very few people in the world know of it. So I am asking those of you who have seen the Light, heard the Sound, and benefited spiritually from your contact with ECK, to let others know about It in your own way.

Sometimes you will do it by example, without ever speaking about ECK. Other times you'll listen to a person who has a tale of sorrow. You'll just be there as a friend; you may not even mention the word ECK.

But if you are ever asked, or if you ever feel the occasion is right, tell these people about HU. Tell them, "Sing HU. Maybe it can heal your heart."

The Light that you carry spiritually from this seminar will go home with you and to all corners of this world. As you go, be aware that you are a channel for God; you carry the love of God with you in your heart, and it's always there.

I'm always with you.

ECK European Seminar, The Hague, The Netherlands, Sunday, July 21, 1991

Both the ECKist and the Muslim magistrate recognized that there was something greater than one's personal religion, and that is to have divine love and respect for another child of God.

17

A Better Friend of the Mahanta

This is the largest ECK seminar that has ever taken place. In a crowd this size, we must be more considerate and full of love than usual.

I know that many of you helped to make this theater presentable for all the guests and visitors here today. You even took the time to cut the grass and clean the grounds to make them as beautiful as we see them now.

People Who Are Ready for ECK

This is the Year of the Vahana, the year of the missionary, and with it we begin a ten-year effort to find the people who are ready for ECK.

An ECKist told me a story that describes the kind of people you will meet as a missionary for ECK. He had a dream that he was in a football stadium, watchful and ready to serve the Mahanta. The Mahanta appeared to him not as Wah Z but as a friend the ECKist knew well.

Bean Cake

"Take these bean cakes," the friend said. "Put them in your bucket and give them to the people."

"There are so many people, I need to have more bean cakes," the ECKist said.

But the Mahanta, in the disguise of the man's friend, merely repeated, "Take these bean cakes and give them to the people."

The ECKist began to argue. He saw so many people that he was sure it would take that many bean cakes.

But the Master said, "Take these bean cakes I have given you and go among the people."

The ECKist went into the crowd of spectators in the football stadium. The first group of people he saw seemed to know that he was coming. They turned and came to him and took the bean cakes from his bucket.

He then saw a second group, but he had to tap these people on the shoulder to get their attention. "Oh, yes, we'll have some bean cake," they said.

It was more difficult to give the bean cake to the third group of people. Even when he touched them on the shoulder, they barely noticed him.

The fourth group was so interested in the game that they had no time at all for his bean cakes.

Food of Soul

Upon awakening, the ECK initiate wondered what his dream meant. He went into contemplation to try to gain an understanding. There he saw clearly that his friend was really the Mahanta, and the bean cakes were the food of Soul.

He realized that the first group represented people who were ready for ECK. The second group had already heard about ECK, but not too much. Once they heard of it, they were quite interested.

234

Most of the people who made up the third group were members of another religion who had heard a little about ECK. They needed a bit more encouragement through the missionary work of ECK. The initiate knew he would have to use a lot of patience.

The fourth group were so interested in the things of this world or so absorbed in their own religion, that they had no use for ECK at all. To these people he gave compassion.

A Witness for ECK

There are many ways to be a better friend of the Mahanta. An ECKist who is a lawyer went to court with a client. The magistrate, a Muslim, asked each party if he would swear to tell the truth, and during the questioning process it came out that the attorney was in ECKANKAR.

The magistrate was a very open-minded man. He said, "I know you are following a natural religion, and I wish I could do the same."

The attorney took the opportunity to mention that there were a total of four people in the courtroom who were in ECK. This is an example of how a person can be a witness for ECK, no matter where he is.

The admission evoked a feeling of friendship between the ECKist and the Muslim magistrate. Both individuals recognized that there was something greater than one's personal religion, and that is to have divine love and respect for another child of God.

Being in ECK does not guarantee that we won't have troubles the same as Christians or Muslims. The reason people are in any religion is to gain spiritual purification. It is through this cleansing by Divine Spirit, or ECK, that they become able to hold more love within them.

Unusual Protection

An ECKist here in Africa was at work one morning when he got a surprise visit from his wife. She was carrying their oldest child. The young girl had received a severe electrical shock earlier that morning.

"A live wire fell on her," the wife explained. "But because the electricity was still coursing through it, no one dared to touch her or try to help. She had to lay there with the wire on her for ten minutes."

When someone finally figured out how to turn off the electricity, the girl was able to get up. The mother took her to the father's place of employment, and from there they rushed her to the hospital. "The doctors were amazed that she was still alive," the father said.

This is an example of how the Mahanta is a friend to you.

School Party

Another case involves a mother and her three small children. The local school was planning an end-of-the-year party for the students. The mother was among the parents who had volunteered to help with last-minute preparations.

"Don't go outside," she instructed the children as she left the house. "In just a little while someone will come with a car and drive you to the school."

But the children were eager to get to the party. After their mother left, the six-year-old boy dressed his younger brother, four, and his baby sister, one and a half. When they were all ready to go, he carefully locked the door behind him and they set out for the school.

The only problem was that the boy was used to having

a bus pick him up and take him to the rural school every day. He soon discovered that he didn't know the entire route.

The children walked along the road until they came to the highway. The oldest boy, not knowing where to go from there, led his brother and sister along the side of the highway. The cars sped by so fast that the children didn't dare attempt to cross to the other side. The sun was hot, and they soon grew tired.

A former neighbor of the family happened to drive by and see three small kids ambling along by themselves. He thought he recognized the oldest boy. Though he feared it might be dangerous to try to stop in the speeding traffic, he couldn't leave them out there all alone.

Luckily he was able to pull off to the side and get to the children. "Where are you going?" he asked them. They told him about the school party. "I'll take you there," he offered.

The neighbor drove them to the school and presented them to their shocked mother. When he explained where he had found them, she became tearful as she realized all the things that could have happened to them. Needless to say, she was very grateful to the neighbor, and the Mahanta, for delivering them safely to her.

Flowers for Mahanta

A Nigerian ECKist, a businessman, travels on occasion to South America. On a recent trip, he and several associates from Nigeria had reservations at a certain hotel. The others knew from past experience that the owner's youngest sister had a prejudice against colored people, especially blacks. Whenever this group of black businessmen checked into the hotel, she was very rude to them.

As the ECKist reflected on the troubled place he was staying in, his thoughts turned to the Mahanta. Suddenly it occurred to him that he would like to buy flowers for the Mahanta, if he could.

In silent conversation he asked the Mahanta, "May I buy flowers for you?"

"Buy them for yourself," the Master answered.

"I cannot buy them for myself," the man said. "That would be selfish."

"Buy them anyway," said the Master.

On Sunday morning he went for a stroll and found that all the stores were closed except for a fruit market. He stopped to buy some apples, then noticed a boy selling flowers. He bought two roses and carried them back to the hotel, wondering to whom he could give them.

All of a sudden he got a strong urge to press the flowers to his heart. As soon as they touched him, he immediately felt the warm love of the Mahanta. "I must be imagining the warmth of the Mahanta from the touch of these roses," he said to himself. So he put a rose to his heart again, and this time he nearly began to cry with love and joy.

Inwardly he heard the Mahanta say, "Because you were willing to buy these flowers, you showed me that you were willing to open your heart to me."

The ECKist now had two very special roses. He thought about giving them to his associates but doubted that they would appreciate such a gift.

Returning to the hotel, he ran into the owner's youngest sister. "Good morning," he said politely. She hissed something back at him, then turned and went into the TV room.

The ECKist took the two roses into the TV room and began to put them in a glass of water. When the owner's sister saw what he was doing, her manner quickly changed from cold to warm. Smiling, she came up to him and asked, "Are those flowers for me?"

"They're for everybody," he said.

"That's all right," she said. "Let me help you put them in water."

For the rest of their stay, the woman was very cordial to the African visitors. One of the other businessmen commented to the ECKist, "I've come here for three years, and this is the first time she has ever spoken to me." The ECKist realized then that the love of the Mahanta can reach even the hardest heart.

These stories will be easy to remember when you go home. Take one story at a time into contemplation, and put your attention lightly on it. This will help you to find its greater meaning.

Spiritual Health

An ECKist has several children. One of her sons became very ill, but when she saw that he was better by the following morning, she decided to go downstairs to her private room to do a Spiritual Exercise of ECK. "I need quiet, so please don't disturb me," she told the children.

She usually reads a passage from *The Shariyat-Ki-Sugmad* as her seed of contemplation. But just as she got settled, her son came into the room. "Mother, may I do the spiritual exercise with you?" he asked.

"Sure," she said. Wrapping a blanket around the two of them, she put aside *The Shariyat* and read to him from one of the ECK youth study books. Then they began to sing HU.

As they sat there, the mother got an insight concerning her son's condition. She had been so busy lately that she hadn't spent enough time with him, and that was likely the reason he had become ill.

At the same time, she realized the care with which the Mahanta looked after her spiritual health. She saw then that she needed to make time to care for her loved ones just as the Mahanta cared for her.

A Better Friend of the Mahanta

How can you be a better friend of the Mahanta? First, carry out the will of the Mahanta, because it's always given with love. The Mahanta will never ask you to harm anyone or anything. If an inner voice tells you to harm another, then it is not the Mahanta. The Mahanta wants only to show you how to open yourself to the love of God.

Secondly, when you go out as a missionary for ECK, remember the four different kinds of people you will meet. Some will be ready for ECK from the moment you speak Its name. Others will hear you only after you speak Its name perhaps two times.

The third group will need to hear about ECK three or more times, but they really don't care too much. And the fourth group is not ready for the teachings of ECK at all.

The dreamer in the first story learned that the Master had given him just enough bean cake to accommodate the people who wanted some. Only later did the initiate understand that not all people want this spiritual food.

Please remember that my love is always with you. No matter where you are, spiritually I am always with you.

ECK African Seminar, Lagos, Nigeria,
Saturday, July 27, 1991

Love is perhaps the most important thing that exists anywhere. If you can love your mate, your husband, your wife, a child, or a pet—if you can love something completely and wholly—that is loving God.

18

What Is ECKANKAR? Part 1

What is ECKANKAR? The simplest explanation is just to say that it means to become a Co-worker with God. This is the whole purpose of Soul's existence in the lower worlds: to get all the experience It can through Its day-to-day problems.

I say Soul, but I'm talking about people. I'm talking about you, and I'm talking about me. We go through the problems of our everyday lives and often we wonder, What do these problems mean? Is this a senseless life? Is this a senseless existence? Or is there some meaning to it?

If we look at life from the viewpoint of a divine being, there is a purpose to this existence. We want to get enough experience to someday gain the compassion, the patience, and all the other qualities needed to become a Co-worker with God.

Who Is the Mahanta?

You are referred to as the Mahanta. Who is the Mahanta? And who is the Living ECK Master?

The Mahanta is a state of consciousness. It is a spiritual state of consciousness very much like the Buddha consciousness or the Christ consciousness. The Living ECK Master is the other half of the title *the Mahanta, the Living ECK Master.* This means the outer spiritual teacher, myself. The teachings of ECK speak very directly and very distinctly of the two parts of the Master: the Inner Master and the Outer Master. The Inner Master is the Mahanta, and the Outer Master is the Living ECK Master.

Sometimes the Inner Master is also called the Dream Master. Inwardly I can teach the students of ECK around the world through their dreams. In Africa people have almost an instinctive understanding of how the dream state works and the importance of dreams. Because of this, it is very natural for me to work with people from Africa.

Difficulties of Mastership

What are the difficulties of becoming a Master? How does one Master take over from another Master?

I don't want to say that my life was more difficult than anyone else's. Each person's life is about as difficult as he or she wants it to be. We all have our problems, and sometimes they are almost too much for us. In this way my problems in trying to attain the ECK Mastership were almost too much for me too.

In a general sense, it was hardest learning patience. I knew that some day I was to be in this position and take the message of ECK to people to tell them about the Light and Sound of God. But first I had to learn to take care of my temper. By nature I'm a fiery person. I'm usually very calm, but every so often I get very excited. These are things we have to work with.

We don't try to get rid of our anger and then say, "I no longer have any anger." We try to be in control of it, from the spiritual point of view. That means sometimes I may mock up anger if necessary to drive a point home to someone. Because I am trying to give him a spiritual understanding of something. Maybe I have done everything I could, spoken very clearly and simply. Maybe I have told him, "For your spiritual unfoldment, you must treat other people more kindly." But the person continues to be rude.

The Holy Spirit, the ECK, is the perfect law of life. But more than the perfect law of life, It is perfect love. And so people must first learn Its ways before they can be filled with divine love.

This doesn't exactly answer your question about the difficulties of becoming the Living ECK Master. It's not that I don't have any examples. Perhaps I have too many. It can be a very difficult time, but no more difficult than it would be for another person to go through the problems of his life, because we all can bear only as much as we can bear. And that depends upon our state of consciousness.

ECKANKAR Is a Religion

Is ECKANKAR a religion, and if it is a religion, how is it different from other religions that we are aware of?

ECKANKAR is definitely a religion. It's difficult to say at what point a spiritual teaching becomes a religion. People don't normally think of this. But if they could take themselves back two thousand years to the beginning of Christianity, they'd see that the early Christians weren't called Christians. Christ was not a Christian. Christ was a Jew. This is something that people forget. Christ is the epitome, the role model for all Christians, yet he was a Jew. Many people have never thought of that before.

Christianity developed very slowly over centuries, over

thousands of years. And it is also this way with the teachings of ECK. It happened the same way with the teachings of Buddha. People didn't go around calling the early followers Buddhists; they were just friends of the Buddha. The early disciples of Christ weren't Christians; they were just friends, or disciples, of Christ.

Christ came because he had a teaching. Buddha came because he had a teaching. All these teachers have a teaching that bears directly upon the spiritual lives of people in their everyday work and life. When the teaching is based on divine love, it actually carries a message to people—not just to their minds but to their hearts.

Outer and Inner Sound and Light

Would you explain to us a little bit about ECKANKAR being the religion of the Light and Sound?

I think people take the Light and Sound for granted in this world because we have the sun's light, we have the moon's light. In this room we have lights. We just take light for granted.

All people need sound simply to exist. Sound is not just something that we can hear. It's also a vibration. Our bodies respond to this vibration.

I'm talking about outer sound and light here. But these can only exist because the Light and Sound exist in the higher heavens of God. The saying is, as above so below. We have light and sound here because they already exist in the higher planes.

Sometimes people see the Mahanta, the Inner Master, as simply a Blue Light. Some people probably have seen the Blue Light and have no idea what this means. Often I wear clothes that are a shade of blue simply to symbolize the Blue Light of the Mahanta. This means the Inner

Master is with that person and is giving them spiritual aid. It may happen years before they come in contact with the teachings of ECK.

Sometimes you may hear the sound of a flute, birds singing, or an orchestra playing. These are examples of the sounds you will hear. Sometimes when you're dreaming or when you're just quiet by yourself, these sounds may come. They may come for no reason during your daily life, but they leave you with the feeling of love and joy. These are very important aspects of God, the Light and Sound.

How Important Is Love?

You've mentioned the word love *quite a number of times. How important is love to an individual in the world and how necessary is it for growth or unfoldment?*

Love is perhaps the most important thing that exists anywhere. Light, Sound, and love are all one and the same. The sun exists because God loves us. And so the sun provides food by shining upon the earth and letting things grow. This is a way God's love comes to us through the sun.

The most important love that people can have for God is to love some other human being first. People so often think that human love is not quite as holy or pure as love for God. But that's not true. If you can love your mate, your husband, your wife, a child, or a pet—if you can love something completely and wholly—that is loving God.

Daily Problems

Here in Nigeria we have what a lot of people would refer to as problems. Our economy is going through a rough period. People usually turn to God when there are such problems. How does ECKANKAR help people solve these sorts of daily problems?

247

That's a big question. How can the teachings of ECK help people during very hard financial times, when there is no money?

When we become adults we know if we eat too much ice cream, we get a toothache or we don't feel well. But give an unlimited supply of ice cream to a child, and the child will eat until he becomes ill. Because it tastes so good. In the United States, we went through a period where we had high prosperity. In the 1920s, we had everything. The idea was to let everybody have whatever they wanted. They thought this would be good for the country.

Spiritually, it doesn't work out that way. We hurt ourselves, and we ended up in an economic depression. It took a decade or so to come out of the depression. During this time the government had to become like a father. The children could not handle themselves, and it took a firm government to say, "We will establish a way of working together to solve our problems."

I believe this is what your president is doing. He has a very difficult job, but I know with the support of the people of Nigeria that you can pull yourself out of the economic straits that you find yourself in. The fact is you are doing it right now. It's very difficult, but you are taking very good steps in that direction. And once the country is taken care of, then the needs of the people are taken care of too, because the country and the people must go together.

Guidelines for Living

Various religions have commandments or rules that the followers must abide by. Are there any rules in ECKANKAR that ECKists must follow or observe?

Sometimes when we are loaded down with rules it becomes very difficult to follow them all. Christ said, "Love your neighbor as yourself," instead of giving people rules that really say "Thou shalt not." I think people grow better spiritually when we say, "Love your neighbor as yourself."

What does this mean? Before you can love your neighbor you must first love yourself. You realize that Soul exists because God loves It, and you try to treat other people as Soul, too, because everyone is a light or child of God. So you treat that person that way. This way you can do away with many of these hundreds of rules.

Focus on Strength

We have rules for working with each other. But to make this the main point of a spiritual teaching is to make people think about their weaknesses. And you can't make people strong by putting attention on their weaknesses. But if you put attention on love, that is their strength. That is our strength, because it comes from God.

Television interview, Lagos, Nigeria,
Saturday, July 27, 1991

If people have been helped by the Light and Sound of God, they will want to tell others about it.

19

What Is ECKANKAR? Part 2

T hose of us who grew up with the Christian religion were made to understand that a man either goes to hell or to heaven depending on how much sin he has committed. What is ECKANKAR's concept of sin?

First of all, people are pretty sure of death. It means something to them. They go to funerals and see that a person is not alive. What is missing in that physical body that made that person alive? The answer is Soul. When Soul leaves the body permanently, suddenly that body doesn't move anymore.

Where Do We Go at Death?

The great teachers of the past have told us that at death people go somewhere. The Christian religion has said that if you leave this body permanently through death you go to either heaven or hell. And this is true in a way, but heaven and hell are conditions that we have made for ourselves. In other words, if a person leads a life that definitely shows he has no love in his heart, then when he dies he will go to a place we might call hell. But there is not just one heaven, and there is not just one hell.

251

St. Paul in the New Testament spoke of knowing a man who is caught up even unto the third heaven. Christianity doesn't speak about the first or second heaven. But St. Paul speaks of a man who was caught up unto the third heaven. This is what we sometimes call the Mental Plane. It's a higher heaven. It's for people who have lived very good lives here. They are usually people who are good spiritually in some way. And it doesn't make any difference what station in life they had on earth.

Soul Does Not Die

In other words, you can go to the higher heavens. Beyond the Mental Plane there is the Soul Plane. This is really the first of the heavens that we in ECK are interested in going to. The first heaven right beyond the physical world is the Astral Plane. Then comes the Causal Plane, then the Mental Plane, then the Soul Plane. This is where we are interested in going because it is the highest heaven so far known to people.

Are you saying that man does not die?

Soul does not die. When Soul leaves the physical body permanently, we call this death.

What Is Heaven?

What happens after that?

People have the image that in heaven the streets will be paved with gold, the windows will be framed with precious stones, and everybody will be walking around covered with jewels. But I think this says more about our values on earth than it says about spiritual values. Because in heaven you have no need of gold, silver, jewelry, or gems. Sometimes people create heaven in their own image.

252

In the book Revelation, it speaks of these things. But people do not know how the books of the Bible were put together. Several hundred years after Christianity began, human beings got together to decide which books would go in the Bible and which would not. Some people didn't want the book Revelation; others did.

Revelation tells about one level of heaven, but there are many heavens. There are indeed places where there are jeweled palaces. But in the high heavens Soul exists simply as a body of light and experiences pure joy.

Our Purpose Here

What then is the purpose of creation?

The purpose of creation goes back to the definition of the word *ECKANKAR*. It means "Co-worker with God." People are here to go through life and get their experiences. By having hardships in life we get our rough edges polished off so we can shine, so the true light of Soul may shine. Earth is a place where we become polished, but so also is the first heaven, the second heaven, and the third heaven. These are places where we get experience in many different ways. For instance the musician Mozart at the age of three began playing the harpsichord. Everybody said, "What a smart child." Well, he had some of this experience from before that lifetime.

How to Overcome Fear

If one dies, is that the end of everything? Or does one come back again?

The Hindu religion talks about the wheel of rebirth. You go around and around and around. The problem is, how long do you stay on the wheel? For many, many

253

lifetimes, they say. But in the teachings of ECK, my job is to help people learn of the Light and Sound of God so that they can get off this wheel of rebirth in one lifetime.

There comes a time when there is no more death, when a person has so much divine love inside that there is no more fear. What is this life all about? I would have to say it's about fear and how to overcome it. You have a job, you're afraid of losing your job. You have health, and you're afraid of losing it. Your child is sick, and you're afraid your child won't get any better. Will you have enough to feed your family? These are all fears. The experience in this world seems to be total fear.

But occasionally there come these little beams of light, sunshine shining into our lives. And this is the love of God. When we can fill ourselves with this love of God more and more, finally there is no room in our heart for the darkness of fear. When this happens we have finished the need to live another life on this earth. We can go to the highest heaven and stay there and enjoy the full blessings of God.

When I say *joy, ecstasy,* and *rapture,* these words aren't sufficient to say what life beyond this world is. Each of the higher heavens has more Light and Sound than the physical plane. So when people leave here, most go to the heavens. Very few go to the hells. When you leave this life you go to a place of more light and more love. I think this should be a comfort to people.

Eternal Teachings

Some ECKists claim that ECKANKAR is the oldest religion in the world. If so, how come a lot of people haven't heard about it until recently?

That is a very good question, and I get it often. When we speak about the teachings of ECK, these are the teachings of the Holy Spirit, because ECK is our name for the Holy Spirit. These are the true, high teachings, and they come in different ages.

For instance, the early people in Christianity were acquainted with the teachings of Spirit in Its pure form. Other people who came after them did not have this pure love of God in their hearts as directly as the disciples of Christ. The people who came later began to form the outer teachings of Christianity. They made dogmas and rules, things which are very necessary for an outer teaching. We have them in ECKANKAR too.

The teachings of ECK are the eternal teachings which have existed here for thousands of years. But as time went on perhaps they became more formulated as Christianity, or as one of the other religions such as Hinduism. The early disciples of Christ were not known as Christians. Because there was no Christianity. What was it, then? The teachings of ECK, the Holy Spirit.

Today it has come out in the form of the religion ECKANKAR. Sometime in the future, perhaps a thousand or two thousand years from now, the teachings of ECK will come again to lift people to a new and higher level. Perhaps these ancient teachings of ECK will have an entirely different name then.

What Is God?

Is there some kind of relationship between Christianity and ECKANKAR?

There is the same thread of love, because the teachings of ECK are basically the teachings of love. Where does the word *love* gravitate to? It goes back to what's known in John 1:1 as the Word: "In the beginning was the Word, and the Word was with God, and the Word was

God." This Word is the Holy Spirit. It's the Voice of God. It's not a person; God is not a person either.

What is God? People like to think of the unknowable in terms that we ourselves can know. So we say God must be the oldest, wisest person we know. But the best we can do is speak of God as the Ocean of Love and Mercy. And that is probably not very accurate either. Because God exists in a world beyond human language. The finite human languages cannot describe the eternal and limitless God. So we do the best we can.

Common Bond of Love

Does ECKANKAR have a relationship with the other religions of the world as well?

In the same way, through this common bond of love. As the different religions grew older, there were some terrible things done in the name of the church. Why? They said it was to keep the teachings pure. I really don't know if you can keep the teachings pure by doing the terrible things that were done during the Spanish Inquisition.

People are people. We have people in ECKANKAR too who want to do the job of God for God. Why don't they just let God take care of God's business? But people try to say, "That person does not believe the way I do. Therefore that person is not following God's will." Who's that person to say? I think Christ said that you should first consider the beam in your own eye, before you become concerned about the specks in your neighbors' eyes.

The Spanish Inquisition that went through Europe was all about people taking the specks out of other people's eyes, when they had the biggest beams in their own eyes. They had too many faults themselves, or they would never have committed the torture and the oppression that they did upon other children of God. To me it's inconceivable.

Yet the same kind of man's inhumanity to man goes on today. We saw it in the United States during our period of slavery. Terrible things were done. Abraham Lincoln tried to set people free. Why? Because he recognized everybody is Soul, a light of God. Can Soul be anything other than free? But people being people, the blacks in America did not get their freedom right away. In the 1960s we had another attempt to get the black people their equal rights as human beings. I think we've come a long way in America, but we still have a ways to go.

Tolerance

In other words, ECKANKAR supports religious tolerance?

Absolutely. We have to. But even in ECKANKAR we have people who are sometimes not very tolerant. Now in my position as the spiritual leader, I may see a weakness in a teaching, where it is not the pure teaching of ECK, of the Holy Spirit, as It was in the beginning of all teachings. Then I say what I must say about that religion.

Some people feel I am criticizing the people of the religion, but I'm not. People are people, and people are always looking for the highest—at least spiritually. But when we look at people and how they behave, we sometimes wonder if they have any idea of what the highest is. We treat each other so poorly sometimes. But if we can follow this basic principle of love your neighbor as yourself, I think this would be a much better world. It would be a much better world tomorrow than it is today.

Missionary Effort

A couple of weeks ago I spoke to some ECKists on an ECK missionary program. What is this ECK missionary program all about?

We have to ask finally, What is our purpose here? I mentioned to someone last night that if our only purpose on earth is to sit here and count our money, then it is a life wasted. It would be very sad if this were the only reason we came here.

What is the missionary effort? Well, you either live your whole life selfishly gaining a dollar for yourself, or for a little part of your life, you tell others about something that has helped you spiritually. If people have been helped by the Light and Sound of God they will want to tell others about it. We do this in a gentle way that does not threaten other people.

I have had missionaries knock on my door, and they come in and stay and stay. But this is not what we do. We try to express the love of God through who we are and how we live. This is our missionary program to tell other people about the Light and Sound of God.

ECK Worship Service

Is that why you have the ECK Worship Service? To reach a lot of people just like the Christians do?

Yes. When Christianity began there were no Christian churches, there was no liturgy. People met in synagogues because that was what they were used to doing. It took years before they began to find their own buildings and have their own worship service, something that meant something special to them.

Our worship service also means something special to us. We sing HU, which is another name for God. It's a word that can give people strength and help in their personal life.

We're developing our own worship service, and it's a long slow process for us even as it was for Christianity.

But because this is the space age, it will probably go much faster than it did in the past two thousand years. Communication is so much better today.

A Home for ECKANKAR

You have an ECK Temple in the United States. What is the purpose of that Temple?

Until we had the Temple of ECK we were like a religion without a home. The Catholics have a home in the Vatican. Every religion has a home of some sort. Until you have that home which becomes your Seat of Power, you really won't ever be able to make a place for yourself in this world.

For instance, every government must have a home. Every country must have a home. The same with every religion, and so with us. About a year and a half ago, we built a the Temple of ECK in Minneapolis, Minnesota. It is a place where people can come together and worship in the Light and Sound of God. Many African chelas have been there already. It's almost become the place for us to go, our Mecca, if you will.

Do you have temples in other places, or do you plan to have them?

I think the early Christians could never have imagined what the Christian church would grow into today, and they could never have had any idea of all the churches and cathedrals that were to come later. All we can do now is put a temple where there are people who have a need to come together. Being a new and young religion we do not have the hundreds of thousands of followers that the major religions do. But we are growing very fast, especially here in Africa.

What message do you have for Nigerian ECKists, or African ECKists? And ECKists all over the world? And those who are non-ECKists?

Sing HU to Open Your Heart

If people would trust their hearts and know that if they love God and open their heart—if they love God through loving their neighbor —they will find that God brings help and protection to them in ways that most people don't know.

Students of ECK here in Nigeria have many stories of protection and healing. They are learning the future in their dreams. This is because they have been able to open their hearts to God's love.

The way to do that is to sing HU to yourself. The song goes like this: HU-U-U-U. You just sing this very quietly to yourself or inwardly. You may see the Light of God; it can be a blue light, a white light, a yellow light, or a green light. You can see it many different ways. Or you may hear the sound of tinkling bells, a flute, a full orchestra, or something as simple as a sigh.

But you will be filled with love.

Sing HU, and this may help you open your heart to God's love. Then you will find the miracles happening in your life too.

Television interview, Lagos, Nigeria,
Saturday, July 27, 1991

Glossary

Words set in SMALL CAPS are defined elsewhere in this glossary.

ARAHATA. An experienced and qualified teacher for ECKANKAR classes.

CHELA. A spiritual student.

ECK. The Life Force, the Holy Spirit, or Audible Life Current which sustains all life.

ECKANKAR. Religion of the Light and Sound of God. Also known as the Ancient Science of SOUL TRAVEL. A truly spiritual religion for the individual in modern times, known as the secret path to God via dreams and SOUL TRAVEL. The teachings provide a framework for anyone to explore their own spiritual experiences. Established by Paul Twitchell, the modern-day founder, in 1965.

ECK MASTERS. Spiritual Masters who can assist and protect people in their spiritual studies and travels. The ECK Masters are from a long line of God-Realized SOULS who know the responsibility that goes with spiritual freedom.

HU. The most ancient, secret name for God. The singing of the word HU, pronounced like the word *hue,* is considered a love song to God. It is sung in the ECK Worship Service.

INITIATION. Earned by the ECK member through spiritual unfoldment and service to God. The initiation is a private ceremony in which the individual is linked to the Sound and Light of God.

LIVING ECK MASTER. The title of the spiritual leader of ECKANKAR. His duty is to lead SOULS back to God. The Living ECK Master can assist spiritual students physically as the Outer Master, in the dream state as the Dream Master, and in the spiritual worlds as the

Inner Master. Sri Harold Klemp became the MAHANTA, the Living ECK Master in 1981.

MAHANTA. A title to describe the highest state of God Consciousness on earth, often embodied in the LIVING ECK MASTER. He is the Living Word.

PLANES. The levels of heaven, such as the Astral, Causal, Mental, Etheric, and Soul planes.

SATSANG. A class in which students of ECK study a monthly lesson from ECKANKAR.

THE SHARIYAT-KI-SUGMAD. The sacred scriptures of ECKANKAR. The scriptures are comprised of twelve volumes in the spiritual worlds. The first two were transcribed from the inner PLANES by Paul Twitchell, modern-day founder of ECKANKAR.

SOUL. The True Self. The inner, most sacred part of each person. Soul exists before birth and lives on after the death of the physical body. As a spark of God, Soul can see, know, and perceive all things. It is the creative center of Its own world.

SOUL TRAVEL. The expansion of consciousness. The ability of SOUL to transcend the physical body and travel into the spiritual worlds of God. Soul Travel is taught only by the LIVING ECK MASTER. It helps people unfold spiritually and can provide proof of the existence of God and life after death.

SOUND AND LIGHT OF ECK. The Holy Spirit. The two aspects through which God appears in the lower worlds. People can experience them by looking and listening within themselves and through SOUL TRAVEL.

SPIRITUAL EXERCISES OF ECK. The daily practice of certain techniques to get us in touch with the Light and Sound of God.

SUGMAD. A sacred name for God. SUGMAD is neither masculine nor feminine; IT is the source of all life.

WAH Z. The spiritual name of Sri Harold Klemp. It means the Secret Doctrine. It is his name in the spiritual worlds.

Index

and seat of power, 11
and responsibility, 56–57
talking to, about ECK, 83–84
Church(es), 58, 65, 161. *See also*
Protestant churches
Cleansing, 193
Clergy, 137
Clerk, 38–41
Cobbler, 162–63
Communication, 222, 228, 229,
231, 259. *See also* Speaking,
public; Talk(s); Writing
Communism, 160
Community, 3, 63–64, 105, 196,
201
Compassion, 58, 235, 243
Competence, 168
Computer(s), 154, 159, 194–96
Confidence, 158, 159
Consciousness
advancing, 23, 33, 92, 107, 147
Christ, 75, 119–20, 169, 170,
244
Cloak of, 169
definition of, 50
dimming the, 23
gaining in, 57, 72, 170
of God's help, 52–53, 184–85
heaven as, 41, 169
improving, 171–72
limits of your, 170
losing in, 170
Mahanta as. *See* Mahanta: as
consciousness
nimble, 10
old, 141
and problems, 51, 245
purified, 144
reflection of, 160
richer in, 181
state (level) of, 10, 60, 83–84,
87, 120
for technology, 159–60
Contemplation, 180, 239. *See
also* Spiritual Exercise(s) of
ECK

Cooperation, 5
Co-worker with God, 35–36,
56–58, 211, 243, 253
Creation, 253
Criticism, 51

Dairy products, 32, 192
Death, 251, 253–54. *See also*
Near-death experience;
Translation
Debt, 136, 163, 168
Deed, good, 17–18, 27, 84
Depression, 248
Despondency, 169
Destruction, 152, 163
Detachment, 131
Diet, 32–33, 190–91. *See also*
Food
Discourse, lost, 129
Discrimination, 185
Disease, 104. *See also* Illness
Dogmas, 255
Doing one thing well, 157–59
Doing your best, 152, 223–25
Donald and Daisy, 155, 176–78
Dove, 142–43
Dream(s)
building a, 26–27
ECK Masters visit in, 13, 197
God speaks through, 185
learning the future in, 260
Master teaches through, 171,
233–34, 244
meeting people in, 70
nature of, 9–10, 69–70
remembering, 69, 71
Dream Master, 69, 244
Drumbeat of time, 198–99
Drum(s). *See* Sound(s) (of God):
of drums
Duck, 176. *See also* Donald and
Daisy

Earth
getting experience on, 71, 253
important time on, 4

265

Earth *(continued)*
  is getting crowded, 156
  leaving this, 211, 254
  our purpose on, 156, 163, 191,
    226, 253, 258
  predictions of end of, 146
  religious conflict on, 84
Earth to God, Come In
    Please . . ., 111
Easter, 123–24
East Germany, 160
ECK. *See also* ECKANKAR;
    Path(s): of ECK; Teaching(s)
  agreement with, 180, 206
  arranges things for the best,
    10, 17, 152
  awake to, 132
  book. *See* ECKANKAR: book
  brings light and joy, 46
  coming into, 162, 193, 211, 230
  discourses. *See* ECKANKAR:
    discourses
  finding, 73–74, 76
  flow, 109
  followers of, 3
  great in, 132
  guidance from, 2, 111, 127,
    128–29, 180
  help from. *See* Help: from the
    ECK
  how the, works, 45–46, 111,
    132
  is love, 108, 144
  life in, 71
  listening to, 181, 184
  manifestation from, 130
  materials, 2
  names for, 94
  nature of, 111
  new spirit in, 127, 130
  new year. *See* New Year, ECK
  open to, 129
  presence of, 59, 119
  purifies, 180, 235
  ready for, 234, 240
  reassurance from, 131

  shutting off from, 102
  speaks to people, 198
  surrender to, 179
  teaches us, 18, 125, 128
  telling others about, 64–65,
    76, 83, 126, 154, 186, 194,
    231, 240. *See also*
    ECKANKAR: talking about
  word of, 2
  works through us, 36. *See also*
    Vehicle
  in the world, 3
ECKANKAR
  book, 2, 74, 171, 186. *See also*
    Book of ECK Parables, The,
    Volume 3; *Earth to God,*
    Come In Please . . .; HU book
    story; *Shariyat-Ki-Sugmad,*
    The; Temple of ECK, The
  book discussion, 127
  changes in, 36–38
  and Christianity, 94, 138–43,
    255
  coming into, 93, 185–86
  definition of, 243, 253
  direction of, 1
  discourses, 2, 197, 200. *See*
    also Discourse, lost; *ECK*
    Dream Discourses, The
  establishment of, 12
  founder of. *See* Twitchell, Paul
  growth of, 4–5, 11, 123, 259
  history, 9, 11, 74, 254–55
  home of, 1, 6
  introversion of, 126
  learning in, 46, 119
  and Light and Sound, 138, 246
  and love, 255
  members of, 74, 138
  nature of, 9, 254
  new era for, 11, 12, 125–27,
    200–1
  not ready for, 117, 171, 235, 240
  and other religions, 138, 235,
    257
  as a religion, 126, 245

266

responsive to spiritual needs, 151

and rules, 248–49

Satsang class, 2, 200

and the Seat of Power, 1, 4–5

seminars. See Love (divine): at ECK seminars; Seminar(s)

steps to, 171–72

talking about, 83, 116–17

twenty-fifth anniversary of, 12

validity of, 172

in the world, 6, 12, 28, 201

ECKANKAR Spiritual Center, 126

ECK Dream Discourses, The, 198

ECKist(s)

are individuals, 94

community of, 61–62, 63

experiences of, 111

and giving, 28

nature of, 43, 44

and other religions, 92, 229–30, 235

persecution of, 3

ECK Master(s), 1, 3, 15, 197. *See also* Dream Master; Inner Master; Living ECK Master; Mahanta; Outer Master; Twitchell, Paul; Wah Z; Yaubl Sacabi

ECK teaching(s)

bringing out, 151

clear a path to the, 131, 132

help people, 210, 248

and Light and Sound, 27, 58

and love, 100, 126

and the Master, 244

nature of, 62, 79–80, 254–55

not pushing, 81–82

other masters and, 62

presenting, 126

purpose of, 50

ready for, 169, 171

secret, 169, 171

students of, 180

and surrender. *See* Surrender

telling people about, 156

understanding through, 200

in the world, 1–2, 3, 27, 193

ECK Worship Service, 94, 107, 258

ECK Vidya, 61, 125, 128, 130

Economy, 136

Edgar Cayce group, 172

Effort(s), 108, 130, 156

Emotion(s) (emotional), 114, 144, 179, 180. *See also* Anger (angry)

Energy, 5, 42, 113

Esteem, 224

Ethics, 58

Euphoria, 117

Evolution, 169, 172

Example, being an, 5

Exodus. *See* Bible

Expectations, 69, 161

Experience(s)

gaining, 71

learning from others', 184

of life, 209, 217

meaning of, 200

opens us, 60, 186

purify, 103

as the purpose for life, 56, 57, 243, 253

reaction to, 41

required in order to teach others, 153

and spirituality, 58

Eyes, 186

Failure, 158

Fairness, 131, 132

Faith, 24, 26–27

Family, 85, 137, 239–40. *See also* Child(ren); Marriage; Spouse; Youth

Far Country, 202

Fast-food restaurants, 190–91

Fat, 189–91

267

Fear
of death, 83
and love, 146, 254
of public speaking, 127–28,
130, 137–38
Fixing yourself, 193
Flowers-for-the-Mahanta story,
237–39
Flute. *See* Sound(s) (of God): of
flute
Food. *See also* Bean-cake story;
Cheesecake; Dairy products;
Fast food restaurants; Fat;
Fried foods; Gluten; Horseradish story; Ice cream; Ice-
cream-bar story; Muffins;
Olives; Peanuts; Pies; Potato
chips; Salad bar; Salt; Yeast
on the Astral Plane, 72
and emotions, 46
and health. *See* Health
labels, 152, 190
reaction to, 32–33, 35
spiritual, 65, 85, 233–34, 240
and spirituality, 31
Forces. *See* Nature: forces of;
Negative forces
Freedom, 87, 145, 164
Fried foods, 190–91
Friendship, 224
Future, 128

Game. *See also* Video: games
of life, 13–14
plan, 106
Garden, 64
Geraniums, 208
Gift, 27, 41–42
Give (giving), 24, 44, 197
without expecting a reward,
17, 27, 28
love, 4, 17–18, 27, 64
spiritual, 41
Gluttony, 72, 103, 108
God. *See also* HU: as name for
God

asking, 54, 60, 148, 166
-beings, 108, 163
communication from, 229
Co-worker with. *See* Co-
worker with God
hearing, 145, 147
help from, 50, 52–54, 64, 109,
207
is love, 88, 108, 144, 161
knowledge of, 218
love. *See* Love: God
love of, 84, 95, 117, 166, 218,
247, 254, 260
nature of, 87–88, 91, 138,
194–95, 228–29, 256
not telling, what to do, 95, 166
one, 87, 91
path to. *See* Path(s): to God
presence of, 211
protection from, 260
relationship with, 88–89, 94,
143, 159, 160
returning to, 66, 191
speaks to us, 61, 139, 140, 142,
143, 159, 160, 185, 228
surrender to, 168
trying to possess, 147–48
Voice of. *See* Voice (of God)
will of, 54, 95, 166, 195, 229,
256
within you, 195
God-Realization, 106
Golden-tongued Wisdom, 61
Goodness, 28
Goose, 175
Government, 248
Gratitude, 36, 167
Greatness, 132, 225, 227
Greed, 165, 169
Grocery shopping, 152
Growth, 50, 159, 180

Hairshirts, 166
Hallucinations, 82–83
Happy (happiness). *See also*
Unhappiness

Human (beings) (race) *(continued)*
  consciousness, 92, 139, 228
  good and bad in each, 227
  impulses, 180
  nature, 147
  need others, 63
  opinions of, 70, 128
  relations, 153
  vanity of, 88, 91, 155
  vision of God, 87
  weakness, 224–25, 249
Humanity, 2, 227
Humility, 18, 164–65, 168, 227
Humor, 102, 155

Ice cream, 191, 192
Ice-cream-bar story, 44
Ideals, 132
Ignorance, spiritual, 77
Illness, 31, 59, 75, 239–40. *See also* Back problems, Bronchitis; Cancer; Parkinson's disease
Illusions, 10
Immigrants, 158–59
Immune system, 191
Individual, 87, 94
Infatuation, 164
Initiates, 3, 12, 126. *See also* ECKist(s); Higher Initiate(s)
Initiation, 41–42, 105, 199
Initiative, 108–9
Inner
  experience, 23, 69–70
  hearing, 217
  planes, 201
Inner Master, 15, 171, 180, 229, 244, 246–47. *See also* Mahanta
Insight, 119, 120, 128
Insurance, medical, 104
Intelligence, 129, 167
Intolerance, 164
Introversion, 126
Intuition, 185, 222
Iron, scorched, 185–86, 192–93, 200

Iron Curtain, 156, 160
Islam, 172
Israelites, 140–42

Japanese tourist story, 54–55
Jehovah's Witness, 118–19
Jesus Christ. *See also* Consciousness: Christ
  baptism of, 142
  and Christianity, 245–46, 255
  disciples of, 92, 246, 255
  and Easter, 123–24
  and the end of the world, 146
  and love, 160–61
  teachings of, 60, 169, 246, 249, 256
  visualizing, 83, 84, 94
  was a Jew, 245
Journal, spiritual, 127, 129
Journey, 209, 214, 217
Joy, 46, 247, 253

Karma (karmic)
  Law of, 14
  lifelong, 77
  nature of, 57, 226
  problems, 186
  taking on others', 78
  understanding, 210–11
  working off, 77, 230
Kinesthesiologist, 32–33
Kingdom of God, 169
Knowing, 56, 222
Knowledge, 72, 129, 218
Krishna, 169

Label, 117
Language, 256
Laughter, 153, 155, 157, 165
Laurel and Hardy, 155
Law(s)
  of Divine Spirit, 78
  of ECK, 180
  of Economy, 77
  of the Holy Spirit, 72
  of Karma. *See* Karma

271

Love (divine) *(continued)*
  bridge to, 108
  and Christianity, 161, 255
  comes from God, 161, 249
  connection with, 169
  ECK, 130. *See also* ECK: is
    Love
  and ECKANKAR. *See*
    ECKANKAR: and love
  at ECK seminars, 109
  expressing, 117, 258
  and fear, 146, 254
  feel the, 100, 112, 116
  filled with, 59–60, 94, 211,
    218, 229, 235, 245, 254, 260
  finding, 58–59, 147, 164, 169,
    229
  giving, 36, 64, 84–85, 94, 144
  God, 100, 167, 247, 260
  human, 144, 247
  and humility. *See* Humility
  importance of, 247
  is limitless, 85
  lack of, 102–3, 108, 229, 251
  learning to, 144, 167
  life, 126, 167
  as light, 254
  and the Light and Sound, 144,
    247
  of the Master, 132
  opening to, 60, 145, 147, 169,
    240, 260
  others, 65, 81, 235
  from others, 74, 100, 106, 109,
    115
  as path to heaven, 16–17
  and power, 163–64
  practicing, 180
  rejuvenates, 136
  relationships, 161, 164
  something more than yourself,
    151, 164
  telling others about, 65, 186
  we carry, 231
  what you do, 100, 152
  yearning for, 107

  your neighbor, 249, 257, 260
  yourself, 161, 165, 249
Loyalty, 59
Lust, 165
Luther, Martin, 160–61
Lutherans, 91, 92
Lying, 108

Magic, 77
Magician, 178–79
Mahanta. *See also* Inner Master;
    Wah Z
  accepting, 81
  asking the, 180
  cares for us, 240
  connection with, 231
  as consciousness, 75, 119–20,
    169, 222, 243–44
  experience with, 233–35
  friend of, 235, 240
  help from, 222, 236–37
  love of, 238–39
  nature of, 244
  relying on, 193
  seen as Blue Light. *See* Light
    (of God): Blue
  teaches us, 184
  voice of, 32, 228
  will of, 240
Malaria pills, 212–13, 221
Mall, shopping, 181–84
Marigolds, 38–41, 208–9
Marriage, 153–54, 160–61, 164
Master(s) (mastership), 84, 171,
    244–45. *See also* ECK
    Master(s); Inner Master;
    Living ECK Master;
    Mahanta; Outer Master
Material possessions, 107
Maturity, spiritual, 179–80
Meddling, 102
Memories, 132
Men, 97, 99
Message
  of ECK, 12, 66, 70, 146, 194,
    196, 244

from God, 92, 135, 138
to the heart, 246
Methuselah, 141
Milo of Crotona, 78
Mind, 70, 165, 167
Minnesota
Chanhassen, 1, 6, 9, 11
Minneapolis–St. Paul, 6
Miracles, 61, 260
Mirror, 51
Mission(ary)
decade of, 193, 233
ECK, 6, 12, 27, 235, 240
effort, 201, 258
for the Holy Spirit, 27–28
joy of ECK, 126
living your, 154
program, 257
and Temple of ECK, 5, 6
Year of ECK, 65, 73, 81
Moment, 127
Monastery, 57
Money, 162–63, 210, 248, 258.
See also One hundred
dollars
Monuments, 132
Mood, blue, 75, 76
Moralists, 164
Mormons, 62
Moses, 139–41
Mozart, Wolfgang, 225–28,
253
Muffins, 190
Mundane, 156
Muscle testing, 32–33
Music, 138, 144
of God, 225–28. *See also*
Sound(s) (of God)
Muslim, 18, 235
Myths, 132

Nations, 11
Nature
agreement with, 209
forces of, 77, 78
Near-death experience, 23, 93

Needs. *See* Spiritual(ity): needs
Negative forces, 222
New Year, ECK, 43
Newton, John, 145
Nigeria, 247–48
Nudge, 127
Nut, 116–17
Nutritionist, 32

Obstacles, 10, 106. *See also*
Problem(s)
Ocean of Love and Mercy, 202,
228, 256
Off track, 102
Olives, 34, 35
One hundred dollars, 22–27
Openness, 129
Opinions, 70, 161, 214
Opportunity, 218
Orchestra. *See* Sound(s) (of God):
of an orchestra
Outer Master, 171, 244
Overview, 131, 201

Parables, 60. *See also Book of*
ECK Parables, The, Vol-
ume 3
Parking (lot), 112–16, 165 – 66,
182–84
Parkinson's disease, 82
Passions, 72, 165–66. *See also*
Anger (angry); Greed;
Vanity
Past, 127
Past life (lives), 58, 128, 167,
180, 197, 199–200
Path(s)
allowing others their, 64,
171–72, 230
of ECK, 69, 211, 218
to God, 108, 161, 169
on our own, 87, 94
spiritual, 78, 85, 230
Patience, 132, 235, 243, 244
Peace, 156
Peanuts, 190

275

How to Take the Next Step on Your Spiritual Journey

Find your own answers to questions about your past, present, and future through the ancient wisdom of ECKANKAR. Take the next bold step on your spiritual journey.

ECKANKAR can show you why special attention from God is neither random nor only for a few saints. It is for anyone who opens his heart to Divine Spirit, the Light and Sound of God.

Are you looking for the secrets of life and the afterlife? Sri Harold Klemp, today's spiritual leader of ECKANKAR, and Paul Twitchell, its modern-day founder, have written a series of monthly discourses that give unique Spiritual Exercises of ECK. They can lead you in a direct way to God. Those who join ECKANKAR, Religion of the Light and Sound of God, can receive these monthly discourses.

As a Member of ECKANKAR You'll Discover

1. The most direct route home to God through the ECK teachings of the Light and Sound. Plus the opportunity to gain wisdom, charity, and spiritual freedom in this lifetime through the ECK initiations.
2. The spiritual meaning of dreams, Soul Travel techniques, and ways to establish a personal relationship with Divine Spirit through study of monthly discourses. These discourses are for the entire family. You may study them alone at home or in a class with others.
3. Secrets of self-mastery in a Wisdom Note and articles by the Living ECK Master in the *Mystic World,* a quarterly newsletter. In it are also letters and articles from ECK members around the world.
4. Upcoming ECK seminars and other activities worldwide, new study materials from ECKANKAR, and more, in special mailings. Join the excitement. Have the fulfilling experience of attending major ECK seminars!
5. The joy of the ECK Satsang (discourse study) experience in classes and book discussions. Share spiritual experiences and find answers to your questions about the ECK teachings.

How to Find Out More

To request membership in ECKANKAR using your credit card (or for a free booklet on membership) call (612) 544-0066, weekdays, between 8:00 a.m. and 5:00 p.m., central time. Or write to: ECKANKAR, Att: Information, P.O. Box 27300, Minneapolis, MN 55427 U.S.A.

Introductory Books on ECKANKAR

We Come as Eagles, Mahanta Transcripts, Book 9
Harold Klemp

Harold Klemp, spiritual leader of ECKANKAR, tells how to discover your greatness as Soul. Learn to understand the spiritual laws of life. The power of divine love can bring spiritual healing, stop nightmares, and show you when God is speaking.

ECKANKAR—Ancient Wisdom for Today

Are you one of the millions who have heard God speak to you through a profound spiritual experience? This introductory book will show you how dreams, Soul Travel, and experiences with past lives are ways God speaks to you. An entertaining, easy-to-read approach to ECKANKAR. Reading this little book can give you new perspectives on your spiritual life.

The Spiritual Exercises of ECK
Harold Klemp

This book is a staircase with 131 steps. It's a special staircase, because you don't have to climb all the steps to get to the top. Each step is a spiritual exercise, a way to help you explore your inner worlds. And what awaits you at the top? The doorway to spiritual freedom, self-mastery, wisdom, and love.

HU: A Love Song to God
(Audiocassette)

Learn how to sing an ancient name for God, HU (pronounced like the word *hue*). A wonderful introduction to ECKANKAR, this two-tape set is designed to help listeners of any religious or philosophical background benefit from the gifts of the Holy Spirit. It includes an explanation of the HU, stories about how Divine Spirit works in daily life, and exercises to uplift you spiritually.

For fastest service, phone (612) 544-0066 weekdays between 8 a.m. and 5 p.m., central time, to request books using your credit card, or look under **ECKANKAR** in your phone book for an ECKANKAR Center near you. Or write: **ECKANKAR, Att: Information, P.O. Box 27300, Minneapolis, MN 55427 U.S.A.**

There May Be an
ECKANKAR Study Group near You

ECKANKAR offers a variety of local and international activities for the spiritual seeker. With hundreds of study groups worldwide, ECKANKAR is near you! Many areas have ECKANKAR Centers where you can browse through the books in a quiet, unpressured environment, talk with others who share an interest in this ancient teaching, and attend beginning discussion classes on how to gain the attributes of Soul: wisdom, power, love, and freedom.

Around the world, ECKANKAR study groups offer special one-day or weekend seminars on the basic teachings of ECKANKAR. Check your phone book under **ECKANKAR**, or call **(612) 544-0066** for membership information and the location of the ECKANKAR Center or study group nearest you. Or write **ECKANKAR, Att: Information, P.O. Box 27300, Minneapolis, MN 55427 U.S.A.**

☐ Please send me information on the nearest ECKANKAR discussion or study group in my area.

☐ Please send me more information about membership in ECKANKAR, which includes a twelve-month spiritual study.

Please type or print clearly   815

Name _____

Street _____ Apt. # _____

City _____ State/Prov. _____

ZIP/Postal Code _____ Country _____